{ **The Secrets to Good Credit and Debt Reduction**

Revised & Updated!

The Secrets to Good Credit and Debt Reduction

Revised & Updated!

A Consumer Self-Help Guide

D. J. Williams

Premier Educational Services, LLC
ST. LOUIS, MISSOURI

© 2001 Deborah J. Williams. Printed and bound in the United States of America. All rights reserved. No part of this book may be reproduced or transmitted in any form or by any means, electronic or mechanical, including photocopying, recording, or by an information storage and retrieval system—except by a reviewer who may quote brief passages in a review to be printed in a magazine, newspaper, or on the Web—without permission in writing from the publisher. For information, please contact Premier Educational Services, LLC, PO Box 771491, St. Louis, MO 63177.

This publication is not intended to provide financial or legal advice. It contains information for educational purposes only. Consult a relevant professional for expert advice. This publication was written with timely and accurate information in regards to the subject matter. The accuracy of the information is not guaranteed, as the laws and regulations are subject to change without notice. Therefore, check the laws of your state before acting. We assume no responsibility for errors, inaccuracies, omissions, or any inconsistency herein. Any slights of people, places, or organizations are unintentional.

ATTENTION CORPORATIONS, UNIVERSITIES, COLLEGES, AND PROFESSIONAL ORGANIZATIONS: Quantity discounts are available on bulk purchases of this book for educational, gift purposes, or as premiums for increasing magazine subscriptions or renewals. Special books or book excerpts can also be created to fit specific needs. For information, please contact Premier Educational Services, LLC, PO Box 771491, St. Louis, MO 63177; ph. 314-436-4002.

1st Edition (ISBN 978-0-9703037-0-7)
    1st printing 2001; 2nd printing 2007
Revised & Updated Edition (ISBN 978-0-9703037-1-4)
    1st printing 2012

Publisher's Cataloging-in-Publication
(Provided by Quality Books, Inc.)

Williams, D. J. (Deborah Jean)
    The secrets to good credit and debt reduction : a consumer self-help guide / D. J. Williams. — 1st ed.
    p. cm.
    Includes bibliographical references and index.
    LCCN: 00-106241
    ISBN: 978-0-9703037-1-4

    1.Consumer credit—United States—Handbooks, manuals, etc. 2. Finance, Personal—United States—Handbooks, manuals, etc. 3. Credit ratings—United States. I. Title.

HG3756.U54.W55 2000   332.7'43
                                QBI00-723

Dedication

This book is dedicated to my son for making me proud, my companion for his loving support, my mother, who was a constant source of inspiration, and my grandmother, who always told me to pay my bills on time and to save a dime out of every dollar.

Acknowledgments

I would like to thank John Weir and Orand Jones for their support and help in bringing this book back to life. I would also like to thank the hundreds of credit counseling clients, borrowers, and real estate agents who placed their confidence in me. I have had the distinct pleasure of working with people of all races, creeds, and colors. Entrepreneurs, doctors, nurses, hospital personnel, lawyers, engineers, principals, teachers, teachers' aides, bus drivers, police officers, firefighters, retirees, cooks, government workers, sales people, manufacturing workers…I could go on and on!

Contents

Introduction ix
How to Use This Book xiii

Part I. Understanding Credit

Chapter 1   *What Is Credit?* 3
Chapter 2   *The Credit System* 5
Chapter 3   *Credit Is Important to Your Life* 7
Chapter 4   *What Is a Credit Report?* 11
Chapter 5   *How to Read Your Credit Report* 15
Chapter 6   *Credit Scoring* 21
Chapter 7   *Know Your Rights* 25
Chapter 8   *Credit Problems Are Not Okay* 29

Part II. Establishing a Good Credit Rating

Chapter 9   *How to Establish Credit* 35
Chapter 10   *Credit Repair Companies* 39

Chapter 11　*Collection Agencies* 45

Chapter 12　*How to Repair Your Credit* 53

Chapter 13　*Protecting Your Credit* 67

Part III. Getting Out of Debt

Chapter 14　*Strategies to Reduce Debt* 73

Part IV. Credit and Purchasing a Home

Chapter 15　*A Stress-Free Loan Process* 85

Conclusion 93

Resources 95

Terms You Need to Know 97

Index 103

Introduction

So much has happened since I first wrote this little book in 2001. My husband of twenty-three years passed away. My son, who was eight then, is now a freshman in college. At that time I was on a mission to educate consumers about predatory lending and the dangers of buying homes with bad credit and no money. What I feared has happened. The writing was all over the wall on a micro level. I just didn't know the effects were going to be global and would nearly destroy our economy. People were buying homes with no jobs, no money, bad credit, teaser rate financing 2/28 or 3/27, pay option ARMS with negative amortization, and stated documentation loans. The mortgage financing environment was like the wild, wild west. Predatory and subprime lenders were running rampant. Everyone and anyone was originating mortgage loans. Just to show you how bad things were from my perspective: One Monday morning I was at St. Louis City Hall taking care of something mundane the city requires of its citizens every year. I got on the elevator with a gentleman in a letter carrier uniform. He struck up a conversation and asked me what I did for a living, and I shared with him my background in banking. He said he was a mortgage loan officer on the side, and my response before I knew it was: "But you are a mailman!" That's just how bad the industry had gotten:

The mailman was originating mortgage loans. Well, we all know that foreclosures are at an all-time high. Households and communities have been devastated. We are now back to basics, and your credit score is more valuable than your net worth.

With financial principles, the more things change, the more they tend to stay the same. The major recent change has been that our credit scores are no longer a secret. Ninety percent of this book has not been changed for the new edition.

This consumer self-help guide is a result of many years of experience, education, and blessings. As you read it, consider it a journey of discovery toward your financial well being. Creating new habits is the key to accomplishing this goal. For thirteen years my career, which was also my research, has been in real estate finance. I worked for regional banking institutions and national mortgage companies. I have a Bachelor of Science degree in special education and a Master's in Business Administration. My mother and my grandparents were entrepreneurs, and I have always had a natural curiosity about how people relate to money. For as long as I can remember I have always wanted to be a teacher. Writing this book is a realization for me that teachers are not just in traditional classrooms. Teachers are everywhere.

Several months after I started my career in real estate finance, it occurred to me there was a tremendous need for financial and credit literacy, and if I was going to be successful, I had to be a good salesperson and a great teacher. I also realized the information I taught made a difference in the lives of people long after our business relationship had ended. Writing this book was a complete labor of love that gives me the opportunity to share vital knowledge to help you achieve your financial goals with ease. I know it is a cliché but *knowledge is power!*

I have been blessed with the opportunity to participate in the lives of many people in the quest to realize their dreams of homeownership. I have learned some valuable lessons. The most important one is that success and failure are relative. I have seen people emotionally devastated because they were denied the opportunity to purchase what they considered the only home for them. Later they discovered what they thought was a setback was an opportunity for growth and the acquisition of benefits that could last a lifetime. This is success!

I've encountered a wide variety of people and circumstances. I have hundreds of success stories. One story in particular that stays with me is of a woman in her forties who applied for a loan to purchase her first home. We established a friendship right away. She had some financial and credit problems that she did not realize would stop her from being able to borrow the money she needed to purchase the house. Before her loan package was submitted for a decision, we met and I pointed out the strengths and weaknesses of the loan package. I discussed with her what needed to be done and how to strengthen her weaknesses. We prayed for a miracle.

Her loan was denied. I called her at home with the bad news. She was not surprised. She said to me, "I know exactly what I need to do. You have shared information with me that I never knew. Don't worry. I'll be back." She did exactly what she said she was going to do. She reestablished a good credit rating, organized her finances, came back as an "A" customer, and borrowed the money she needed to purchase a home.

Seven years later she called me to make an appointment. Her property had appreciated significantly with the improvements she had made. She was selling it and buying another. With her excellent credit history, little debt, and money to make a nice down payment, she easily qualified. I was pleased to see her achieve her financial goals with ease. She said to me, "You taught me well, I feel free. I just wish I had learned the value of credit earlier in my life."

Current lending practices and the kind of story you just read inspired me and ultimately led me to write this book. As you travel through this book, spend time at each section and understand the importance of your journey. Make stops that best suit your situation. If you have good credit and too much debt, go directly to Part III, Getting Out of Debt. If you have a bad credit history, stop off at chapter 8, Credit Problems Are Not Okay. Then go directly to Part II, Establishing a Good Credit Rating. If you have never had credit, pay particular attention to chapter 9, How to Establish Credit. If you are thinking about purchasing a home go to Part IV, Credit and Purchasing a Home.

Good luck! And remember good credit is not an option—it's a must!

How to Use This Book

Congratulations! You have made the first step toward financial freedom. A good credit rating is your most valuable asset. Without good credit, legally you can be charged higher interest rates for your home and automobile purchases. Without good credit, you may pay more or are denied major purchases, employment opportunities, apartments, and insurance for yourself and your family.

A home, employment, insurance, automobiles, furniture, appliances, and so forth are essential to living a balanced life. With a bad credit rating, you can be denied these essentials. A bad credit rating negatively affects the financial lives of families and individuals. It is very important that you understand how credit affects your life and why it is so important that you do not have bad credit.

This book is designed to give you a broad and basic knowledge of credit and debt. You can expect to learn how credit and debt affect your choices and overall attitudes, and how to establish and maintain a good credit rating. The chapters are brief for easy reading. There is plenty of space for note taking. Discuss the book with your family, friends, and coworkers. Give it as a gift to others who are just starting out, experiencing credit problems, have filed bankruptcy, or are in bondage with too much debt.

You will encounter many detours on the road to discovering good credit. This book will help you make informed decisions. To prepare for this journey you must do two things:

First, read the Terms You Need to Know section in the back of the book. Second, order your credit report from each of the three major credit-reporting agencies. It is important that you have your credit reports in front of you while you make this journey. To be able to actually look at your credit report while you go through this book will help you tremendously.

Part I of this book was designed to increase your knowledge of the credit system and the role credit plays in your life. After reading Part I you should be able to do the following:
- Understand the credit system
- Read a credit report
- Understand credit scoring and how it's used
- Know your rights as a consumer
- Understand why credit problems are *not* okay

Parts II and III are designed as workbooks to guide you through the following processes:
- Establishing credit
- Repairing and updating your credit report
- Dealing effectively with collection agencies and credit repair companies
- Getting out of debt

Part IV will help take the mystery out of applying for a loan to purchase a home. Knowing what to expect and being prepared is 90 percent of what you need to take the stress out of the loan process.

If you are willing to make a commitment to yourself and to getting your credit in order, you will soon experience financial freedom that will last a lifetime.

Part I

Understanding Credit

"When wisdom entereth into your heart and knowledge is pleasant to your soul.... Discretion shall preserve you and understanding shall keep you"

(Proverbs 2:10–11)

Chapter 1

What Is Credit?

Credit is based on the Latin word *creditum*, meaning trust or faith—an expression of trust in you and your promise to pay in the future for merchandise purchased or money borrowed. This expression of trust is not money and it is not free. You pay interest or finance charges for the privilege of using credit.

Credit is critical to the national economy as well as your household economy. Credit has become an important part of all phases of today's life and its importance continues to grow. Working capital for businesses, automobiles, and home purchases would not be possible without credit. Credit has made outstanding contributions to the development of the U.S. economy and to the high standard of living enjoyed by many Americans.

Credit and credit needs are growing. Approximately half of what we purchase as consumers and 90 percent of all business expenses involve credit. We have many uses for credit: home and car purchases, repairing and improving our homes, starting businesses, and making investments. Its importance cannot be overemphasized. If used wisely, it can help make dreams come true. Traditionally, business and industry have emphasized that personal credit is a privilege, not a right. For instance, you may have the right to buy a house, but if you need to borrow the money to do so, the lender has the right to set the rules for borrowing the money. Businesses have become increasingly favorable toward the use of consumer credit. Businesses know that the acceptance of credit from consumers gives them a competitive edge by which to expand sales, profits, and market share. Most consumers use credit for one or all of the following reasons: to raise their standard of living, to increase their enjoyment of life, and for necessity and convenience.

Thus the challenge to us is to have a complete and clear understanding of the rules of credit and what it can and cannot do for us. Remember, fortunes have been made with the wise use of credit. The wise use of credit—not debt—is what this book advocates. Everyone should be able to use credit when he or she needs it. Believe me, sooner or later 99 percent of us will have a need to use credit for one reason or another.

Points to Remember
- Credit is an expression of trust in you and your ability to pay in the future for money borrowed or purchases made.
- Credit is being used for convenience, out of necessity, to raise the standard of living and to enjoy life.
- Credit is vital to the nation's economy as well as your household economy.
- The purchase of homes, cars, and working capital for businesses would not be possible without credit.
- Fortunes have been made using credit wisely.

Chapter 2

The Credit System

We live in an economic system driven by private production and private ownership, known as capitalism. Capitalism operates on individual production (employment or self-employment) to create private ownership of resources, goods, and other things (money, businesses, houses, automobiles, investments, and so forth).

Many debate the fairness of capitalism. Is there really equality of opportunity for everyone? Why do some have so much and others so little? Whether capitalism is a fair economic system or the best system, it is the only game in town. To be successful, you must play the game and win. You win if you have good credit and little debt. You lose if you have bad credit and/or a lot of unnecessary debt. Understand the rules. The money you earn must be managed and leveraged with the wise use of credit in order to succeed in a capitalist society.

The credit-reporting system is the gatekeeper to full participation in a capitalist economic system. It allows some to enter the good life and keeps others in financial turmoil. Encountering the credit system is the first hurdle you are presented with when you move toward private ownership. Whether it's business or consumer credit, you must have these doors open to you, or you cannot fully participate in a capitalist society. Once you have an understanding of the credit system and know the importance of having good credit, you will be able to move through this system with ease.

The credit system operates on several levels. It allows individuals with good credit to acquire and build personal wealth. It can be used to take advantage of individuals with bad credit. It also allows those with good credit to get into financial difficulty by becoming overwhelmed with debt. The choice is yours. You make the decision how the credit system will work for you.

This decision will have a great influence on the way you live your life. The wise use of good credit allows you freedom. Freedom to make choices that are beneficial to you—freedom to dream and to have dreams come true. Whether your dreams are homeownership, becoming an entrepreneur, or investing your money, understanding the credit system and establishing good credit can play a major role in helping you realize your dreams.

Points to Remember
- Capitalism allows individuals to create their own private wealth.
- Sooner or later everyone participates in the credit system.
- You make the choice how the credit system will work for you.
- Good credit opens doors to full participation in the credit system.
- Bad credit closes some doors and opens others that are exploitive and predatory.
- The wise use of credit can make dreams come true.

Chapter 3

Credit Is Important to Your Life

Credit problems can have a negative effect on your life.

Health

Financial wellness is essential to you and your family's mental and physical health. Credit problems cause stress in your life, and stress causes all kinds of physical and mental problems. Are you always facing a financial crisis in your life? Do you always worry about money? Are you always playing "catch up" with your bills? Are you considering bankruptcy? Have you already filed bankruptcy? When you are burdened with a bad credit rating, you are repeatedly denied access to credit. To be denied access to credit jeopardizes other areas of your life like access to shelter, an apartment, or a house.

Too much debt is also very stressful. You experience a lack of freedom when you are burdened with too much debt. This can lead to irrational behavior and inappropriate decisions. A good credit rating and low debt is very important to your mental and physical well being.

Divorce

Divorce can be the result of financial problems, and divorce can cause financial problems for both parties. Credit problems have destroyed many families. There are a couple of points to keep in mind: First, you are responsible for individual debts. These are usually the credit cards and/or loans you had prior to getting married. If it is an individual account then that individual is the only one legally responsible for the bill. In community property states both spouses can be held responsible for separate non-marital debt.

Both parties are responsible for joint accounts, that is, accounts you both signed for, such as mortgages, car loans, credit cards, and so forth. A divorce does not change joint liabilities. The lender extended credit or made a loan to both of you and both of you are equally liable for the debts. The only entity that can release one party of liability is the lender that extended the credit, not the divorce attorney or judge.

Employment

Imagine that for three months you have been employed at a great company through a temporary agency. You really like the job and the work environment. You are offered a full-time permanent position with a good salary and benefits. While signing "new hire" papers in the human resources office, you notice they require your signature to get a credit report. How's your credit rating? Do you know what is being reported on you? Although not all employers require a credit check, what happens when the job you want does? What if you are being considered for a promotion and they require a credit check? Will your credit report help or hurt you?

As you can see, credit is very important to your life and can have devastating effects when you neglect it.

Points to Remember
- Credit problems cause stress in your life.
- Your general well being is jeopardized when you have credit problems.
- Credit problems can break up marriages.
- You can be denied a place to live because of your credit history and be forced to settle for a less desirable dwelling.
- Too much debt compels you to make decisions that are not in your best interest.
- You can be denied employment or promotions because of your credit history.

Chapter 4

What Is a Credit Report?

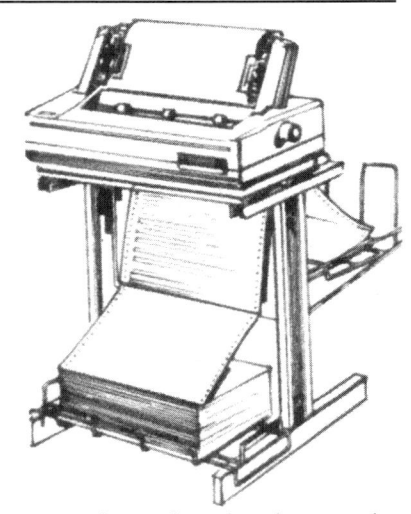

Also known as consumer reports and credit checks, credit reports are documented records of background information and credit activity or inactivity on every individual with a social security number in this country. The credit system issues credit reports to determine our level of performance as adults and consumers, just as the education system issues grade reports to determine our level of academic performance.

We can't discuss credit reports without discussing credit-reporting agencies or credit bureaus. A credit-reporting agency gathers information such as where you live and work, what legal actions have been filed, what bills you have, and how you pay those bills. This information about you is then sold to creditors, employers, insurers, and other businesses. Credit-reporting agencies are private businesses. They are not government agencies. The Fair Credit Reporting Act (FCRA), amended by the Fair and Accurate Credit Transaction Act (FACTA), is enforced by the Federal Trade Commission (FTC) and your state attorney general. It clearly states how credit-reporting agencies must conduct their business and what your rights are as a consumer (see chapter 7, Know Your Rights).

Credit reporting works in this manner. Let's use Sears department stores as an example. Sears subscribes to the services of the three major credit bureaus: Equifax, TransUnion, and Experian. Sears reports to the credit bureau on a monthly basis the payment history of every customer who has an account with them. The credit bureau keeps a file on you and records in your file every month what Sears reports to them. When an employer or creditors ask to see your credit file, the credit bureau generates a credit report. The credit report assists employers, creditors, and insurers with the decision-making process. So if you have three credit cards, a car loan, and so forth, each one is reporting your payment history to a credit bureau. This information will be added to your file. Creditors, employers, and insurers receive this information on a daily basis.

Assumptions concerning your character are made by examining your credit history. Most people are not aware just how much the credit report reveals about them and their habits. Here are some examples of information that is available:

- You have been employed for ten years at the same job.
- You have not paid a three-hundred-dollar bill you have owed for over three years.
- Your last landlord filed a judgment against you for past due rent.
- You have had a car loan for two years and every payment, with the exception of three, has been more than thirty days late.
- Your wages are being garnished for unpaid obligations.
- You have filed bankruptcy.

Creditors and employers use this information to approve or deny your loans, credit cards, employment, insurance, and other requests.

Remember that credit-reporting agencies compile and report the information provided to them by creditors (banks, credit cards companies, and so forth.). They don't create information.

That is why they are called "reporting" agencies. They only report what is provided to them. But they do make mistakes and so does the creditor reporting the information. It is up to you to correct the mistakes in your credit file. With FACTA you are entitled to a free credit report from all three credit bureaus once a year. Go to www.annualcreditreport.com. Seven out of ten credit reports have errors. If you do not correct your credit file, your report will have mistakes that could be detrimental to you and your credit score. The FCRA states that a credit bureau cannot report any information about a consumer that is not true, accurate, and verifiable. All negative information that is obsolete (seven years old plus 180 days after the account first became delinquent) must be deleted from your file. The credit bureau must be able to verify the information is true and accurate or it must be removed from your file. (Remember this when we discuss credit repair.)

Generally, all credit reports have the following information:

- Background information: your first, middle (or initial) and last name. Aliases, if any. Current and previous addresses, social security number, date of birth, current and previous employment, date hired, your position, and sometimes your income.
- Credit information: details of credit activity, information on credit cards, auto loans, mortgages, student loans, installment loans, and so forth. This information includes the names of creditors, account numbers, types of accounts (joint, individual, cosigned, or authorized user), date the account was opened, loan amount, credit limit, current balance, and terms (number of payments and payment amount).
- Credit history:

    Historical status—the number of months the creditor has reviewed the account and the number of times the applicant has been thirty, sixty, or ninety days late with payment

    Last past due—the date when the account was last past due

    Collections—accounts that were not paid, then were submitted to collection agencies

Public record information—obtained from the local, state, and federal courts; contains bankruptcy records, foreclosures, tax liens for unpaid taxes, judgments, and child support arrearage

Inquiries—names of creditors that have obtained a copy of your credit report and how often you have applied for credit

Points to Remember
- Credit reports are also known as consumer reports and credit checks.
- All credit reports contain background, account, and credit history information.
- Credit-reporting agencies are also referred to as credit bureaus.
- Credit-reporting agencies report information provided to them by creditors.
- Credit-reporting agencies sell credit reports to creditors, landlords, collection agencies, insurance companies, mortgage companies, and employers.
- The FCRA and FACTA govern how the credit reporting agencies conducts business.
- Credit reports can reveal character traits.

Chapter 5

How to Read Your Credit Report

Reading credit reports can be confusing to anyone who is not accustomed to reading them. I wish I had a dollar for every time I've heard "I can't read this thing." Unfortunately, there are people working in credit-granting businesses who also misinterpret credit reports. The credit report is full of codes and symbols. The law requires credit bureaus to provide the key to the codes and symbols with every report. The law also requires the credit bureau to provide staff who can help you understand your report. However, over the last decade credit reports have become more consumer friendly.

It is important that you are able to read and interpret your own report. Otherwise, how will you know what information is being reported on you and if that information is accurate? The reports may look different but they all contain the same information: your background information, credit information, and credit history.

Let's locate the following information on your credit report. You will always find this information at the top of your report.

Background information

Name: Age:
Marital status: Social security number:
AKA:
Co-applicant name: Age:
Marital status: Social security number:
AKA:
Current address: How long?
Previous address: How long?
Dependents:

The following information is either mixed in with the background information or in a separate section following the background. On some reports all previous information, such as previous address and previous employment, are located on the last page of the report.

Employment information

Applicant's employer: City: State:
Position: Income: Date hired:
Previous employer:
Position: Income: Dates:
Co-applicant's employer: City: State:
Position: Income: Date hired:
Previous employer:
Position:

Credit history

- *Creditor*—name of bank, credit card company, mortgage company, collection company, and so forth.
- *Account number*—number assigned to your account by creditor.
- *Date verified*—the date when this information was last updated. Check this date first to make sure your information is current.

How to Read Your Credit Report   17

- *Date open*—date you opened the account.
- *High credit*—highest amount you ever owed on the account.
- *Balance owing*—current balance on the account.
- *Amount past due*—amount currently past due on the account.
- *Terms*—number of payments and payment amount.
- *ECOA*—(Equal Credit Opportunity Act) who is responsible for payment of debt. This code (ECOA) indicates who is responsible for each account and the type of participation for that account. Here are some codes from different credit reporting agency. As you can see, for example a joint account could be coded J, S, or C. Be sure to read the code explanations on the back of the credit report you have.

  A—authorized to use someone else's account
  I—individual account
  J—joint account or joint contractual liability
  S—shared (joint account)
  S—cosigner, no spousal relationship
  B—cosigner (responsible only in case of default on the account)
  C—co-maker (joint responsibility of account)
  M—maker (individual account)
  M—cosigner primarily liable for account
  T—terminated account
  U—undesignated (creditor did not designate)

- *Type of account*—the first letter represents the type of account, a number following the letter represents MOP (manner of payment), for example, I-1 or R-1.

  R or REV—revolving
  I or INS—installment
  O or Opn—open thirty days
  M or MTG—mortgage
  C or CRL—line of credit
  Y or Col—collection

- *MOP* (manner of payment)—how the account is rated; shows the credit rating on each account

  0   too new to rate
  1   pays (or paid) within thirty days of billing, pays account as agreed

- 2 pays (or paid) in more than thirty days but not more than sixty days, or not more than one payment past due
- 3 pays (or paid) in more than sixty days, but not more that ninety days, or two payments past due
- 4 pays (or paid) in more that 90 days, but not more that 120 days, or three or more payments past due
- 5 pays (or paid) in 120 days or more
- 6 pays (or paid) in 150 days or more
- 7 wage earner plan/bankruptcy—WEP/BKRP
- 8 repossession or foreclosure—REPO/FCL
- 8A voluntary repossession
- 8D legal repossession
- 8R repossession redeemed
- 9 collection account and charged off to bad debt
- UR unrated

- *Past due*—number of times payments received thirty, sixty, and ninety days late as reported by the creditor.
- *Last past due*—the last time you were past due on the account.
- *Mos. rev.*—months reviewed, the number of months of credit history the creditor has provided. For example, if the mos. rev. shows sixty and there is a one in the thirty-day column, on this account you have been thirty days late, one time in a sixty-month period.
- *Collection accounts, public records information (judgments and bankruptcy), and inquiries* are usually found at the end of the report.

Now that you have read the codes and know what they mean, go back to each section and circle all the information that's not current and incorrect. This is the time to do some preliminary work for repairing your credit report.

Check for the correct spelling of your name. If you have a common name, be sure to add your middle name. Check your social security number and date of birth. Make sure they are reporting your current address and employer. Your credit report can show you living and working somewhere you have not been in years. Establishing stability is important.

Go through the credit history and make sure account numbers, balances, and terms (monthly payment) are correct. If you have a cosigned account on your report, be sure it's coded correctly under ECOA. You don't want a cosigned loan coded as an individual account. I have seen many situations where a person thought he or she had cosigned for a loan and the creditor had actually made them the primary borrower. This means you are totally responsible for this debt.

Pay close attention to the MOP section. This is where your credit is rated according to the manner in which you pay your bills. Start taking notes on this section. You will have a majority of the work done when you get to chapter 12, How to Repair Your Credit. Check for the accuracy of late payments. Remember that this refers to payments that have been made thirty days after the due date. Make note of accounts that have amounts in the past due column if the account is current. This is an account that has not been updated. Check the last date the account was verified.

If you have collections and judgments that have been paid, make sure your credit report shows they have been paid and that the date and year are listed correctly. You don't want a collection or judgment filed in September 1996 to show paid in December 1999 when actually it was paid in December 1996. This happens frequently, especially when you are dealing with local courts and public records. This is so important because you don't want to give a creditor the impression you ignored an obligation for three years when actually you paid the bill right away.

Points to Remember
- Don't be intimidated by the codes and symbols on your credit report.
- Study your credit report until you are sure of what is indicated about your credit history.
- If you are not sure what your credit history indicates, call the credit bureau and have them explain it to you.
- Note outdated and inaccurate information.

Chapter 6

Credit Scoring

This chapter will answer your questions on credit scoring.

What is credit scoring? It's your credit report reduced to a three-digit number ranging from 350 to 850 and sometimes as high as 900. This score is used to determine the cost and risk involved in extending credit to you. What is the likelihood of you repaying a credit obligation as agreed? The lower the score, the greater the risk you are for a creditor, and the more likely you will be denied a loan or end up paying more in interest.

How are credit scores calculated? A statistical program is used to perform research into credit patterns that predict credit performance. Points are assigned to factors of your credit information such as: payment history (how you have paid current and previous accounts), outstanding debt (the number of account balances compared to the total credit limits; the rule of thumb is to keep your credit balance at not more than 30 percent of your credit limit), credit history (how long you have had credit), types of creditors (mortgages, installment loans, revolving credit, bank cards, payday loans, and so forth), credit inquires (request for your credit report). This information is compared to the actual credit performance of consumers with similar profiles. Points are awarded for each factor that helps predict who is most likely to repay the loan on time. It is not good enough to just pay back. You must pay on time! The total number of points is your credit score.

How can I get my credit score? Just a couple of years ago our credit scores were a secret and were only available to creditors who subscribed to the software packages that generated the scores. Today, everywhere you look on the web, someone is trying to sell our credit score to us either through a credit monitoring service or a credit reporting agency. For a fee you can get your credit score from any one of the three credit reporting agencies. The FICO score is the most common one used by creditors. You can get this score with your Equifax credit report (for a fee, of course), or you can go to www.myFico.com and buy just your score. TransUnion and Experian also offer their own credit scores. Note: Credit scores do not come with the free credit reports from www.annualcreditreport.com.

What makes credit scores objective? Credit scoring is considered an objective tool because race, sex, age, marital status, national origin, religion, and income cannot be used as point factors to create the credit score.

What is a good credit score? Acceptable credit scores vary from industry to industry. What is acceptable for an insurance premium may not be acceptable for a mortgage or an auto loan. Prior to the economic recession, 660 and above was considered a pretty good score. Now, above 700 is considered a good score. With risk-based lending, you can get credit with a score between 640 and 660. Below 620 is considered a high risk.

How old is credit scoring? Credit scores were first developed and used in the consumer finance industry back in the l950s. For many years credit scores have been used to determine credit worthiness for credit cards and auto loans.

Why are lenders now using credit scores more? It is considered a quick and objective method for evaluating a credit report to predict who is more likely to repay a loan. Lenders are accused of being unfair and subjective in their credit granting decisions. Credit scores are considered fair and objective because they are based on real data and statistics of millions of consumers.

Are credit scores the reason you can get credit cards, auto loans, and home loans so quickly? Yes. Credit scoring allows lenders to make credit decisions faster and over the Internet.

Should I be concerned about my credit score? Yes. It's your financial reputation and can cost you thousands of dollars and peace of mind—not to mention your dreams. If you keep a good credit rating, manage your debt and monitor your credit report, you will have a good credit score.

If my credit report is not accurate, will this effect my credit score? Credit scoring is the reason why it is imperative that you make sure your credit report is accurate and up to date. It is your responsibility to make sure your credit report is accurate. If you don't do it, no one else will. There are other factors that are considered to approve or deny a loan. Most mortgage lenders will tell you they do not approve or deny mortgage loans based on credit score alone.

Can you improve your credit score? Yes. Consistency is key! Start paying your bills on time! Lower your debt and avoid collections and other legal actions such as judgments and bankruptcy. You cannot change the past but you can change the future.

Points to Remember

- A credit score is a tool used by lenders to quickly evaluate the credit report and predict the risk factor.
- Credit scoring is one reason it is so important to make sure your credit report is accurate and up-to-date.
- Credit scores are widely used in every industry today.
- Lenders consider credit scores accurate predictors of loan performance across all income groups.
- Credit scores cannot be easily changed.
- The wise use of credit and consistent on time payments will raise a low credit score.

Chapter 7

Know Your Rights

The Fair Credit Reporting Act, with the amendment known as The Fair and Accurate Credit Transaction Act, is a federal law that protects you by regulating how consumer credit reports can be used and obtained. You have important rights because of the FCRA.

The law gives you the following rights:

- You have the right to know exactly what is in your credit file and what is being reported on you. But only if you ask for it! Don't say you don't want to see it. You need to know what is being reported on you, good or bad!
- You have the right to a free copy of your credit report from each of the nationwide credit reporting agencies, Experian, TransUnion, and Equifax, at your request once every twelve months.
- You have the right to a free copy of your credit report within sixty days of being denied credit.

- You have the right to know the name and address of the credit bureau responsible for preparing the credit report used to deny you credit, insurance, or employment, or to increase the cost of your insurance or credit.
- You have the right to a free copy of your report if you are unemployed, a recipient of public welfare assistance, or believe you have been the victim of fraud.
- You have the right to understand your credit report.
- You have the right to a complete and accurate credit report.
- You have the right to dispute information on your credit report. The credit bureau must investigate your dispute within thirty days.
- You have the right to dispute any information on your credit report that is not true and accurate.
- You have the right to have all incorrect information deleted from your credit report.
- You have the right to have all information that cannot be verified deleted from your credit report.
- You have the right to have all those who received incorrect information notified at no cost to you.
- You have the right to a fresh start, with negative information deleted from your file after seven years plus 180 days after your account first became delinquent.
- You have the right to have a Chapter 7 bankruptcy deleted from your file after ten years. For Chapter 13 you have to wait seven years.
- You have the right to know the nature, substance, and sources of the information in your credit file.
- You have the right to know who received your credit report in the last six months for credit-granting purposes.
- You have the right to inform the credit-reporting agency that it may not supply information about you to your employer or a prospective employer without your consent.
- You have the right to know who has seen your credit report in the last two years for employment purposes.

- You have the right to review your credit file in person and to have an attorney, family, or friend with you.
- You have the right to tell your side of the story and include a one-hundred-word consumer statement regarding any dispute as a permanent part of your credit report.
- You have the right to be notified by a company that has requested an investigative report about you.
- You have the right to know the nature and the substance of the investigative report but not the sources.
- You have the right to request from the company pursuing an investigative report more information about the nature and scope of the investigation.
- You have the right to have your name removed from "preapproved" mailing lists.
- You have the right to confidentiality.
- You may have the right to sue the credit bureau.

Points to Remember

- You are entitled to an accurate and up-to-date credit report.
- You have the right to understand your credit report.
- You have the right to dispute any information on your credit report that is not true and accurate.
- You have the right to have any information that cannot be verified removed from your credit report.
- You have the right to a fresh start after seven years.
- You have the right to have a bankruptcy deleted from your file after 10 years.
- You have the right to expect any information you dispute to be investigated within 30 days.
- You have the right to a free credit report within sixty days of being denied credit.

Chapter 8

Credit Problems Are Not Okay!

When you see the words "credit problems okay," *stop* and proceed with caution. *Credit problems are not okay!*

Why are people with credit problems targeted? Legally, they can be charged higher interest rates and finance charges because they are considered high risk by some lenders. Therefore, it can be very profitable to address the financial needs of consumers with credit problems. Also, consumers with credit problems don't have many options, leaving them vulnerable to abusive legal and illegal credit practices.

What is predatory lending? Lenders who target consumers with credit problems for abusive loan practices. Consumers with credit problems and homeowners with substantial equity in their properties can be prime targets, as well as consumers purchasing homes or borrowing money for some urgent need. With credit problems you are the prey these lenders pursue.

What do you mean by abusive loan practices? Loans with high interest rates; high points and high closing costs; "balloon payments;" loan flipping (multiple loans on the same property); high prepayment penalties; selling and financing overpriced credit, life, and disability insurance; and many other practices that are not in the best interest of the borrower.

Why is predatory lending a problem? Predatory lending is a national problem because the abusive loan practices target low to moderate income borrowers, women, and the elderly. These practices result in a substantial increase in foreclosures and the destabilization of neighborhoods, a decline in property values, and many destroyed lives.

What is subprime credit? It is for borrowers who do not meet the traditional credit criteria, those with low credit scores and considered high risks. Higher insurance premiums, deposits for utilities, higher interest rates for auto financing, mortgages, pay day loans, and title loans are all examples of subprime credit.

What are prepayment penalties? You pay a penalty for paying the loan off early. For example, for a $50,000 mortgage loan with a 2 percent prepayment penalty, that is $1,000 in addition to other costs to pay the loan off. This provides additional profits and can lock the borrower into this loan for a longer period of time if they can't pay the prepayment penalty.

What is loan flipping? Loan flipping is repeatedly refinancing a loan by continuing to roll it over into a new loan and repeatedly charge the same high fees and high interest rates each time the loan is refinanced. There are documented cases of borrowers who had eleven loans with one lender over a four-year period.

What is the advance-fee loan scam? Lenders or individuals claim they can guarantee you a loan regardless of your credit, for a fee paid in advance. The fee can range from $100 to several hundred dollars. Small businesses can pay as much as several thousand dollars advance fees for a loan.

What options do people with credit problems have? Not many! If you want furniture or appliances the "rent to own" stores where you can pay double the cost are available, or the higher interest-rate neighborhood furniture stores may be your only option. If you need to borrow small sums of money, your options include family, friends, pay-day loans, check advance loans, and car title loans, for which you will pay unreasonable interest rates. Today, buying a house is much more difficult with a low credit score, whereas people with good credit are taking advantage of the lowest interest rates in history.

If good credit is a requirement to financial freedom, why do we see "credit problems okay" advertised? As you can see, credit problems are only okay for some to exploit you and make money as a result of your problems.

Points to Remember
- It is not okay to have bad credit.
- Consumers with bad credit are targeted for abusive loan practices.
- Credit problems limit your ability to acquire consumer products and services at market rates.
- It is best to reestablish a good credit rating before applying for credit.

Part II

Establishing a Good Credit Rating

"And let us not be weary in well doing for in due season we shall reap if we faint not"

(Galatians 6:9)

Chapter 9

How to Establish Credit

Trying to establish credit can be frustrating and tricky. What you have probably learned is if you don't have credit, you can't get credit. Establishing credit can be compared to a baby learning to walk after the crawling stage.

Step 1. The baby stands up with hands out, to get its balance. This is you making the decision to establish a good credit rating.

Step 2. The baby stands and takes the first step. This is you taking the first step of setting up a checking and savings account at a bank or credit union.

Step 3. The baby starts to walk after a few stumbles. This is you on your road to establishing a good credit rating.

Let's explore these steps to establishing a good credit rating:

1. Open a checking and savings account at a credit union or bank. Credit unions are good when you are just starting out because they are smaller and cater to the needs of their members. Banks now have special programs to encourage savings. Do some comparison shopping before opening accounts. Look at the minimum deposit to open an account, the required minimum balance, and the fees, fees, fees!

Make regular deposits to your saving account. Establish a habit of saving. Have money go to your savings automatically every pay period. The deposits can be for as little or as much as you can afford. Get into the habit of doing the adding and subtracting of your money going in and out of your checking account and don't bounce checks. You can only spend the money once. If the teller or ATM balance is more than your check register, then you have checks that have not cleared yet.

This is not only the first step to establishing a good credit rating; it's the first step to managing the money you work so hard to obtain. Do this for six to twelve months before you take the next step.

2. Apply for a Visa or MasterCard (secured or unsecured). A secured credit card requires a savings deposit. The interest rate will be high, but that's the price you pay until you establish a good credit rating. An unsecured credit card does not require a savings deposit. The interest rate will probably be high because you are establishing or reestablishing your credit rating. Take the money from your savings account for the required savings deposit. Make sure you are dealing with a reputable bank. (The name of the bank issuing the card must appear in all advertising. If it says "guaranteed" stay away—nothing is guaranteed before an application is made.) Start using the card by making small purchases, such as gas, and pay the balances off every month with on-time payments. No late payments! Please don't think that your required savings deposit can be used for payments. It cannot. This is insurance for the bank. Remember, your goal is to establish a good credit history by making payments on time and not creating debt. Spend twelve months on this step.
Or

Apply for a small loan. You can usually accomplish this with a credit union. You may get the loan on your signature, or they may use your savings account as security for the loan. Most large banks don't make small loans. Don't borrow from the payday loan stores or finance companies. The interest rates and fees are too high. Once you get the loan, put it in your savings account. This is insurance. You will be able to make on time payments and earn some interest to offset the interest you are paying on the loan. The goal is to establish a good credit history, not to create debt. Again, perform this step for twelve months.

3. *It is advisable to have at least three credit references on your credit report.* Take your Visa or MasterCard and open an instant credit card at one of your local department stores. Use it only to make small purchases that you can pay in full and on time every month.

4. *Always be aware of what companies report to the credit bureau.* Banks, department stores, credit unions, and finance companies usually report to credit bureaus. Cell phone and utility companies don't usually report monthly payment history but provide other perks for good payment histories. They do report negative delinquent accounts. Establish a habit of always paying your bills on time.

Points to Remember
- Checking and savings accounts are vital to establishing credit.
- Make regular deposits to your savings account.
- Don't bounce checks.
- Negotiate a secured credit card if you are unable to get an unsecured credit card.
- Be sure the bank's name is prominent in the advertising for secured credit cards.
- Establish a habit of paying on time.
- You must use the credit card to establish a rating.
- Do not create debt; make small purchases and pay them off every month.

Chapter 10

Credit Repair Companies

Your credit score is your household's most valuable asset. With the country in an economic downturn, people are more likely to seek the services of a credit repair organization.

Credit repair organizations are defined as any company or individual that provides advice or assistance in improving one's consumer credit record, credit history, or credit rating for a fee.

The federal government regulates credit repair organizations. According to the Federal Trade Commission, the Consumer Credit Protection Act was amended to include the Credit Repair Organizations Act because of the following findings made by Congress:

"Consumers have a vital interest in establishing and maintaining their credit worthiness and credit standing in order to obtain and use credit. As a result, consumers who have experienced credit problems may seek assistance from credit repair organizations which offer to improve their credit standing.

"Certain advertising and business practices of some companies engaged in the business of credit repair services have worked a financial hardship upon consumers, particularly those of limited economic means and who are inexperienced in credit matters."

The Credit Repair Organization Act *does not* include the following:

1. A 501(c) (3) nonprofit organizations of the Internal Revenue Code of 1986.
2. A creditor assisting the consumer to restructure any debt owed by the consumer to the creditor.
3. Any bank or credit union.

Credit repair organizations are *prohibited* from the following:

1. Making any statements, or advising or counseling you to make false or misleading statements concerning credit worthiness, credit standing, or credit capacity to credit-reporting bureaus or creditors.
2. Making any statements, counseling or advising you to create a new identification to prevent the reporting of your credit record rating or history for the purpose of concealing negative information that is accurate and not obsolete to credit-reporting bureaus, or creditors.
3. The use of any false or misleading representation of their services.
4. Advance payment for the performance of any services the credit repair organization has agreed to perform before such service is fully performed.

Credit repair organizations are required to provide the following disclosure (separate from any other document) before any contract or agreement between you and the credit repair organization can be executed:

Consumer Credit File Rights Under State and Federal Law

You have a right to dispute inaccurate information in your credit report by contacting the credit bureau directly. However, neither you nor any "credit repair" company or credit repair organization has the right to have accurate, current, and verifiable information removed from your credit report. The credit bureau must remove accurate, negative information from your report only if it is more than 7 years old. Bankruptcy information can be reported for 10 years.

You have a right to obtain a copy of your credit report from a credit bureau. You may be charged a reasonable fee. There is no fee, however, if you have been turned down for credit, employment, insurance, or a rental dwelling because of information in your credit report within the preceding 60 days. The credit bureau must provide someone to help you interpret the information in your credit file. You are entitled to receive a free copy of your credit report if you are unemployed and intend to apply for employment in the next 60 days, if you are a recipient of public welfare assistance, or if you have reason to believe that there is inaccurate information in your credit report due to fraud.

You have a right to sue a credit repair organization that violates the Credit Repair Organization Act. This law prohibits deceptive practices by credit repair organizations.

You have the right to cancel your contract with any credit repair organization for any reason within 3 business days from the date you signed it.

Credit bureaus are required to follow reasonable procedures to ensure that the information they report is accurate. However, mistakes may occur. You may, on your own, notify a credit bureau in writing that you dispute the accuracy of information in your credit file. The credit bureau must then reinvestigate and modify or remove inaccurate or incomplete information.

The credit bureau may not charge any fee for this service. Any pertinent information and copies of all documents you have concerning an error should be given to the credit bureau.

If the credit bureau's reinvestigation does not resolve the dispute to your satisfaction, you may send a brief statement to the credit bureau, to be kept in your file, explaining why you think the record is inaccurate. The credit bureau must include a summary of your statement about disputed information with any report it issues about you.

The Federal Trade Commission regulates credit bureaus and credit repair organizations.

For more information contact: The Public Reference Branch
Federal Trade Commission
Washington, DC 20580

The Credit Repair Organization Act requires written and dated contracts. The contract must contain a full and detailed description of the services performed by the credit repair company for you. It must include all guarantees of performance and the date that the performance of services will be complete or the time frame necessary to perform the services. The terms and conditions of payment should include the total amount of all payments to be made by you to the credit repair company or individual.

The contract also must have the name and address of the company boldly displayed, as well as the following statements: *You may cancel this contract without penalty or obligation at any time before midnight of the 3rd business day after the date on which you signed the contract. See the attached notice of cancellation form for an explanation of this right.* Each contract should have an attached form entitled Notice of Cancellation. If you enter into a contract with a credit repair company, you must be given copies of the contract, disclosures, and any other documents you are required to sign.

Now you know what a credit repair company can and cannot do for you. Also remember what they can do for you, you can do for yourself. However, repairing your credit takes time and effort. You may not have the time or the desire to do it. You may decide to pay someone to do it for you.

Points to Remember

- A credit repair organization can be a company or an individual that charge a fee to repair your credit.
- The Credit Repair Organization Act was enacted to protect consumers from financial hardships by credit repair companies.
- The Credit Repair Organization Act does not regulate the practices of nonprofit organizations, banks, credit unions, or any creditors working with consumers who owe them.
- Credit repair organizations are prohibited from advising you to lie to credit-reporting agencies and creditors.
- Credit repair organizations are prohibited from advising you to create a new identification to conceal negative information that is accurate.
- What a credit repair organization can do for you, you can do for yourself.
- If you choose to utilize the services of a credit repair organization, be an educated consumer.
- In 2008 the Federal Trade Commission closed down thirty-four credit repair organizations for violations of the Credit Repair Organization Act.

Chapter 11

Collection Agencies

Have you experienced collection companies that have called you at work, harassed you at home, and were abusive and deceptive? You do not have to accept these practices from debt collectors. The Fair Debt Collection Practices Act (FDCPA) prohibits debt collectors from such practices.

What is the Fair Debt Collectors Practices Act? Congress amended the Consumer Credit Protection Act with FDCPA to address some critical issues concerning the conduct of debt collection businesses. If these issues were ignored, it could jeopardize the efficiency and effectiveness of the credit system.

What were the critical issues? The exact findings were: "There is abundant evidence of the use of abusive, deceptive and unfair debt collection practices by many debt collectors. Abusive debt collection practices contribute to the number of personal bankruptcies, to marital instability, to the loss of jobs, and to invasion of individual privacy. Existing laws and procedures for redressing these injuries are inadequate to protect consumers."

What is meant by "debt collector"? We know a debt is any obligation to pay money as a result of some type of transaction. A debt collector is any person or persons whose principal business is the collection of debts. These businesses regularly collect or attempt to collect, directly or indirectly, debts due to another party. They are commonly called collection companies.

Does this include collection departments for banks and department stores? No. This amendment does not include employees of a creditor collecting debts in the name of the creditor.

Are there other debt collectors excluded from this amendment? There are several: debt collectors acting on behalf of a partner or corporate affiliate who are not in the debt collection business, an officer or employee of the United States whose official duty it is to collect any debt; any person serving legal papers in connection with a judgment, any nonprofit organization that performs credit counseling and assists with the liquidation of debts, debt collections associated with certain activities such as bona fide fiduciary or escrow agreements, collecting of personal debts, debts obtained as a secured party in a commercial credit transaction, and debts that are not in default at the time the debt was obtained by the collection company.

Are there any restrictions as to how far a collection company can go to locate me? Collection companies are allowed to locate you in order to try and collect the debt. They must adhere to a standard of conduct in locating you and collecting the debt. When a collection company communicates with anyone other than you, they must identify themselves and state specifically that they are confirming or correcting address information on you and if asked, must state whom they represent. They cannot make statements related to debts that you owe. They cannot continue to communicate with that person unless requested to do so or the collection company believes they initially received inaccurate or incomplete location information and that the person now has the accurate information. They cannot communicate by postcard. They cannot use any symbols or language on their stationery that indicates they are in the business of debt collection or the mail being sent to you is related to the collection of a debt. Once you inform the collection company you are represented by an attorney regarding the subject debt, they cannot communicate with anyone other than that attorney. If for some reason the attorney fails to respond to them within a reasonable period of time, the company will contact you.

How are collection companies required to communicate with me? During reasonable hours, collection companies may not communicate with you at any unusual time or place that is known to be inconvenient to you or at your place of employment if they know your employer prohibits you from receiving this type of communication.

Can I stop communications from a collection company? Yes, if you notify the company in writing you refuse to pay the subject debt or you are requesting they stop communicating with you. (This does not relieve you of the obligation if you owe it.) The collection company can no longer communicate with you concerning this debt except to advise you that their efforts are being terminated and to notify you of other remedies.

Can a collection company harass you? A collection company is in violation of the law if it: (1) uses obscene or profane language, (2) uses or threatens the use of violence or other criminal activities to harm a person, or his or her property or reputation, (3) makes a public list of consumers who allegedly refuse to pay debts (This does not include reporting to the credit-reporting agency.), (4) advertises the sale of a debt to coerce payment, (5) causes your telephone to ring or engages you in conversation repeatedly or continuously with the intent to annoy, harass, or abuse, or 6) makes telephone calls without disclosing its identity.

Can a collection company make false or misleading statements to try to collect a debt? No! Collection companies may not use any false, deceptive, or misleading statements or actions in connection with the collection of a debt. The Fair Debt Collection Practices Act cites very specific conduct that is in violation of this act.

What types of false statements or misrepresentations do these companies collecting debts make? There are many. Some say they are bonded or affiliated with the United States or some state; or they represent themselves to be attorneys or imply any communication you received was from an attorney. They cannot represent that nonpayment of debt will result in arrest, imprisonment, and seizure of property or garnishment unless legally they can take this action and intend to do so. They cannot make false representation or implication that documents are legal when they are not or vice versa or misrepresent legal documents saying they do not require any action on your part. They cannot threaten to communicate credit information they know to be false or misrepresent that they are employed by a credit-reporting agency.

Isn't it an unfair practice for a collection company to try to collect more than the original debt? Yes, to try to collect any amount (including interest or expense incidental to the principal obligation) that is not expressly authorized by the agreement creating the debt or permitted by law is a violation of the act.

What are considered unfair practices by collection companies (in violation of the Fair Debt Collection Practices Act) as regards postdated checks? Collection companies cannot solicit postdated checks or other postdated payment instruments for the purpose of threatening or instituting criminal prosecution. They cannot accept checks postdated by more than five days unless you are notified in writing of the intent to deposit the check, not more than ten days or less than three days prior to the deposit. They cannot deposit or threaten to deposit a postdated check prior to the date on the check. Collection companies are also prohibited from causing charges to be made to you for communications under false pretenses, such as, but not limited to, collect telephone calls and telegram fees.

How do I know the debt the collection company claims I owe is valid? Within five days after your initial communication, the collection company must send you a written notification containing: (1) the amount of the debt, (2) the name of the creditor to whom the debt is owed, (3) a statement notifying you that you have thirty days to dispute the validity of the debt or any portion of it (If there is no response, it will be assumed to be a valid debt.), and (4) a statement informing you that, if you notify the collection company in writing within the thirty day period that the debt or a portion of it is disputed, then the collection company will obtain verification of the debt or judgment and mail it to you. The company must also state that you have thirty days to make a written request of the name and address of the original creditor, if different from the current creditor.

What happens while I am trying to obtain validation of a debt? Once you notify the collection company in writing within the thirty-day period that the debt is in dispute, or to request the name and address of the original creditor, the company ceases collection of the debt until it has mailed you verification of the debt or the name and address of the original creditor.

What if I fail to dispute the validity of a debt? The failure to dispute the validity of a debt under this act is not an admission of liability in any court.

Is there civil liability for collection companies that violate the law? Yes. You have the right to sue a collector in a state or federal court within one year of the date of the violation. You may recover for actual damages plus an additional amount, not exceeding $1,000. You may also recover court costs and attorney fees. A class action suit may recover damages up to $500,000, or 1 percent of the collector's net worth.

Do you know of any debt collectors who had to pay for violations of the law? The Federal Trade Commission announced the following in May of 2004: "NCO Group to Pay Largest FCRA Civil Penalty to Date." This is a debt collector that violated the Fair Credit Reporting Act. NCO was ordered to pay $1.5 million to settle the Federal Trade Commission charges.

Exactly what were the charges? According to the FTC complaint and press release, "NCO Group Inc, NCO Financial Systems, Inc, and NCO Portfolio Management, Inc violated the Section 623(a)(5) of the Fair Credit Reporting Act, which specifies that any company that reports information to credit bureaus about a delinquent obligation that has been placed for collection or written off must report the *actual month* and *year* the account first became delinquent. This date is used by the credit bureau to measure the maximum seven-year reporting period the FCRA mandates. This helps to ensure that outdated debts—debts that are beyond this seven-year reporting period—do not appear on the consumers credit report.

The FTC charges that NCO reported accounts using later-than-actual delinquency dates. Reporting later than actual dates may cause negative information to remain on a consumer's credit report beyond the seven-year reporting period permitted by the FCRA for most information. Of course, when this occurs, consumers' credit scores are lowered, resulting in their rejection for credit or having to pay higher interest rates."

Did NCO admit it violated the law? No. The $1.5 million civil penalty consent decree was for settlement purposes only and did not constitute an admission by NCO.

Since NCO did not admit guilt, is it still violating the law? The consent decree permanently bars NCO from reporting later-than-actual delinquency dates to credit bureaus. NCO is required to make sure all reporting errors are corrected quickly.

Where can I report a collector for violations? You can report to your state attorney general's office or the Federal Trade Commission (www.FTC.gov Consumer Complaint).

Points to Remember

- The Fair Debt Collectors Practices Act prohibits collection companies from harassing you.
- The Fair Debt Collectors Practices Act regulates the practices of individuals and companies whose principal business is the collection of debts.
- The Fair Debt Collectors Practice Act does not include the employees of a creditor attempting to collect a debt from you.
- You can stop a collection company from communicating with you.
- Collection companies are prohibited from making false and misleading statements to try to collect a debt.
- A collection company must provide you with proof of the validity of the debt it is attempting to collect.
- Collection companies can violate the Fair Credit Reporting Act by re-aging collection accounts.

Chapter 12

How to Repair Your Credit

"Are you a victim of a poor credit rating?"

Today more than ever it is absolutely essential that you repair your credit rating. Many American consumers have low credit scores for various reasons. A large percentage of these consumers have experienced financial difficulty because of divorce, unemployment, illness, or a failed business. A smaller percentage is due to irresponsibility or a lack of knowledge. Credit problems last much longer than the situations that caused the credit problems. For instance, you are no longer unemployed, but your credit is still "bad." Or you have been divorced for several years and your credit is still "bad." Your bad credit rating stays with you, unless you do something about it. Your credit rating is not something you think about until there is a need for credit or you have been denied credit.

Credit can be denied for weakness in one or all of the following areas:

● Credit rating and low credit scores.

- Qualifying requirements—verifiable, consistent income to support the amount of debt you have.
- Equity investment—how much capital you have; this can vary from savings to equity in a home.

The major ingredient, however, for obtaining credit is your credit rating score. Gone are the times of irresponsible lending and the following consumer ads: "Bad Credit? Bankrupt? We can help. Call toll-free 1-800-XXX-XXXX." "We're looking for the WORST credit. Call 1-800-XXX-XXXX." These were actual advertisements. This phenomenon has had a devastating effect on the economy, individuals, and communities. Today, in order to reach any of your financial goals you will need a credit score above 660 and in most instances 700 and above.

Let's look at some other reasons for credit denials:

- *Delinquent credit obligations*—late payments, collections, charge-off, judgments, and so forth.
- *Credit application incomplete*—the information the creditor needed to make a decision was not provided.
- *Too many inquiries*—each creditor determines the number of inquiries considered for excessive credit activity. The assumption is you are trying desperately to get credit and are being rejected. Creditors are not compassionate, so don't look for an attitude of "maybe we will give them a chance with our money, when everyone else is rejecting them."
- *Insufficient credit file*—not enough credit history. Not all creditors report to the credit bureau; only the creditors that subscribe to the services of the credit bureau, such as banks, credit card companies, mortgage companies, and so forth, do so. If you have credit with a company and they do not report to the credit bureau, request that they report your account to the credit bureau. (There may be a charge for this.) This information will not be updated, however, because they do not normally report.
- *Errors on your report*—the credit report and application do not match. Correcting errors is the first step to take in repairing your credit rating to avoid a credit denial due to errors on your reports.

Start the process of repairing your credit rating before you apply for credit. If you have a bad credit rating, it is absolutely essential that you reestablish a good rating. It is easier to reestablish your credit while you still have open accounts that you are currently paying. Perhaps you have been late or past due, skipped payments, or stopped payments, and although you have the account you can't use it. If possible, bring the account current and start to change your behavior today by paying your bills on time. If it is not possible to bring the account current all at once, set up a payment plan with the creditor and make the payment on time until the account is paid in full. You can't change the past but you can change the future.

The first step toward repairing your credit rating is to get copies of your credit reports. Remember that you are entitled to one free credit report from each of the three major credit bureaus once a year. Simple go to www.annualcreditreport.com. If you can't get them online, mail in the form that's provided for you.

Equifax Credit Bureau
PO Box 740241
Atlanta, GA 30374-0241
800-685-1111

Experian (Formerly TRW Credit Bureau)
PO Box 949
Allen, TX 75013-0949
888-397-3742

Trans Union Corporation
Consumer Disclosure Center
PO Box 390
Springfield, PA 19064-0390
800-916-8800
800-682-7654

After receiving your reports, prepare to start working with the credit bureaus and the creditors that report to the bureaus. Here's how to get started:

- Read and interpret each report from each bureau. Remember that the information on all reports is basically the same but each bureau may use different codes. Be sure to look at the "keys to the code" on the back of each report. Sometimes the key is on a separate sheet of paper. If you still don't understand your report call the customer service department of the credit bureau and ask someone to go over your report with you. The law requires the credit bureau to have staff available to answer any questions related to your credit report.
- Start making notes of inaccurate and old information. Ask the following questions:

  Is all the background information accurate and up-to-date (name, addresses, date of birth, social security number, employment, and so forth)?

  Do all of the accounts listed belong to you? Note those that don't.

  Are the accounts accurate and up-to-date?

  Watch for accounts that have been paid but are still listed as unpaid, accounts not updated in the previous 12 months, old information still on credit report (seven years for negative information), and accounts that were included in a bankruptcy but are not indicated as such. Remember NCO and look for collection accounts with dates that are not accurate.

Now you are ready to work with the credit bureau to remove, and correct and update information on your credit report. Remember the following points when working with the credit bureaus: The credit-reporting agency has thirty days (beginning on the date the agency receives written notice of a dispute) to investigate any disputes.

- The credit-reporting agency can report only accurate and verifiable information.
- Disputed information that cannot be verified must be deleted from your report.

- The credit-reporting agency must correct inaccurate information.
- The credit reporting agency must delete any negative accounts that are outdated (seven years plus 180 days from the first date of delinquency).
- The credit-reporting agency must complete all incomplete information. For example, if you have an account that you were late making payments, now you have no past due balance and the account is current.
- The credit-reporting agency must show the complete picture.
- The credit-reporting agency must delete all accounts that do not belong to you.

When the investigation is complete, the credit bureau must give you the results of the investigation in writing and a free credit report if the dispute results in changes to your report.

Once information has been changed or removed, the credit-reporting agency cannot put the disputed information back on your report unless the creditor verifies it is true and accurate. The credit bureau must give you written notice of its intent to put the information back on your credit report.

If you are disputing an item, be sure to provide copies of documents that support your position (paid receipts, letters from companies, copies of applications, and so forth).

It's always a good idea to send a dispute letter and documents to the creditor reporting the inaccurate information. Credit card companies usually provide an address to send disputed information. After receiving your dispute letter, the creditor must note on your report that the account is in dispute. After the investigation and if the information they reported is not correct, the information must be removed. It can never be reported again.

- Send a letter (see sample letter 2, page 64) to each of the three credit bureaus. Each letter should address the inaccuracies being reported on your credit report.
- Keep copies of everything you send and send the letters registered mail with return receipt requested. You must do

this so that you will know the exact date the credit bureau received your letter. Upon receipt of your correspondence, the thirty-day investigation is initiated.
- Wait for the credit bureaus to respond. If you mailed your letters to the three credit bureaus at the same time, you should get responses from the bureaus about the same time. They have thirty days to respond.

During these thirty days, the credit bureau is sending information to the creditors requesting verification of the information you are disputing. Sometimes creditors respond within that time frame, and sometimes they don't. When the creditor does not respond, the credit bureau must remove the disputed item from your credit report because they cannot verify the information as true and accurate. However, when this happens and the creditor verifies the information is true, the credit bureau will notify you that the information is going back on your credit report. Creditors that have accurate negative information that is paid off may not respond, especially for old accounts. Creditors that you still owe will probably respond.

- If you have not heard from the credit bureaus within thirty days, send a follow-up letter (see sample letter 3, page 65).
- Once you have received your updated reports, compare the old ones to the new ones. Review the credit reports individually. They are not the same. You are correcting your credit report with three different credit bureaus. All three credit bureaus should have updated the personal information. What you are looking for is consistency that the accounts listed belong to you and that the history of these accounts is accurate and up-to-date. Make sure this information is consistent with all three bureaus.

Pay attention to negative accounts that you know are true and were deleted from your credit report because of no response from the creditor. Unless the account is seven years old, you might get notification that the account is going back on your credit report. If an account is seven years old

How to Repair Your Credit 59

and unpaid, it will still be removed if it is seven years from the time the account was submitted for collection.
- If you are not satisfied with the accuracy of your reports, repeat the process until you are. Be aware that the credit bureau will not continue to investigate disputes they suspect are "frivolous or irrelevant" and you are using a plan to trigger missed deadlines to have negative information that is true removed from your credit report. The creditor can verify the negative information is true after the deadline, and the credit bureau will then put it back on the report.

Say you have updated your credit report and you still have paid accounts that are listed as negative. If you could get these accounts off your credit report, the report would show a much better credit history. But the creditor continues to update this account. Now is the time to go directly to the creditor. Only the creditor can change how and what they report to the credit bureau. Try the following:

- Call the customer service department. Tell your story to the representative and ask if they can assist you with regaining a good credit rating. Remember that customer service representatives are everyday people that experience some of the same problems. Get the address and a name if possible to make your request in writing.
- Write a letter to the creditor (see sample letter 4, page 65). Be honest and state the reason for the problems with the account. If you have no good reason for the poor payment history of the account, state that you now understand the importance of a good payment history and that is the reason you worked so hard to pay the account in full. State the problems you were experiencing are now in the past and you would like to regain a good credit rating. Provide any documentation you have to support your request.
- Make a follow-up call in seven to ten days. Repeat your story to every customer service representative you contact. Don't be afraid to get another representative involved in your crusade. Find out if your letter was received and what, if any, action has been taken.

- In thirty days, order a credit report and see if the creditor made any changes to your report.
- Repeat the process until you get the results you want. If it becomes obvious the creditor is not going to make any changes or delete the account, that is okay. It does show that the account is paid. The older it gets the less weight it has and eventually it will come off your credit report.

A good current credit history will eventually outweigh a past poor credit history.

Say you have updated your credit report and you still have negative accounts that you owe. You can take the following steps:
- Contact the creditor or the collection agency to negotiate a payoff or repayment plan and to restore a positive credit rating. If the account has gone to a collection agency, try to negotiate with the original creditor. The creditor can be more flexible with their negotiations. Sometimes the creditor will not deal with you after an account has been turned over to a collection agency. Try to avoid having a debt turned over to a collection agency. It can be more difficult to deal with some collection agencies because some agencies consider you a "deadbeat."
- Whether it is the creditor or collection agency, make your initial contact to negotiate a repayment plan. Your plan should be realistic. Don't agree to terms that you can't live up to or that can cause you additional problems. If, for example, the creditor wants $100 a month but it will be difficult for you to pay this, don't agree to it. Whatever you agree to, you must pay on time every month with no late payments. You want to realistically be able to make these payments on time every month.
- Remember when you are negotiating, the agreement must be beneficial to you and the creditor. It must be a "win-win" situation. Some additional points to negotiate are:

If you promise to have the account paid off in a short period of time (one to twelve months), request that the collection agency delete the account from your credit report or give you a better rating if you are paying the creditor directly.

Ask to have the negative rating changed after six months of on-time payments. If you are dealing directly with the creditor, ask to change the status on the account from closed to open and report the on-time payments.

- Try to get the final agreement in writing. If they won't put it in writing, ask if you can fax a letter (see sample letter 5, page 66) verifying the agreement.
- Here is an opportunity for you to reestablish your credit rating. Honor the agreement and make all your payments on time or ahead of time. If for some reason you can't make the payments, call immediately before you miss any payments and discuss your "temporary" situation.
- Request a copy of your credit report to verify your new credit rating. If the creditor didn't honor the agreement, dispute the accuracy of the account with a copy of the letter as documented proof.

Don't forget if you have a good payment history with creditors that do not report to the bureau, such as auto dealers, furniture stores, and so forth., for a fee the credit bureau can add them to your report. Especially if you have been denied credit due to "insufficient credit file" or "no credit file."

We have discussed the majority of the situations that occur on credit reports. You can continue to dispute information on your credit report in an attempt to further clean up your report for as long as you like or until the credit bureau says they consider the disputes to be frivolous.

Realistically, you may not be able to clear all the negative information reported, such as bankruptcies, civil judgments, tax liens, and foreclosures. Be certain to get the releases for all tax liens and judgments and make sure your credit report reflects they are paid.

The good news is you are entitled to a new start every seven years, with the exception of bankruptcies, which will remain on credit reports for ten years.

Keep your current credit good and the past credit will become less significant and eventually be removed.

Points to Remember

- The problems with credit last longer than the situations that caused the credit problems.
- If you don't correct your credit report, no one else will.
- Get a copy of your credit report at least once a year.
- Dispute all inaccurate and outdated information on your credit report.
- The credit bureau has thirty days to investigate your dispute.
- If the credit bureau cannot verify what they are reporting is true and accurate, they must remove it from your credit report.
- Keep copies of everything.
- A good current payment history will eventually replace the poor past payment history.
- Always pay on time.
- Keep your credit card balances under 30 percent of the credit limit.

Sample Letters

These letters are provided as examples of the type of correspondence you can use to communicate with the credit bureau. You may also use the forms the credit bureaus usually provide when they send your credit report. Be sure to read the consumer information included with the credit report.

Sample #1: Request for credit report

(Send to All Three Credit Bureaus)
To: Name of credit bureau
From: Your name
Date: Today's date
Re: Request for credit report

Enclosed please find a check (or money order) in the amount of $X to cover the cost of the credit report.
My full name:
My social security number:
My date of birth:
My current address:
My previous address:

Please send the report to the above current address. Thank you.

Your signature

Sample #1A: Request for free credit report based on a credit denial

To: Name of credit bureau
From: Your name
Date: Today's date
Re: Request for credit report

Please send me a copy of my credit report. I have been denied credit in the past sixty days by (company name). My denial was

based on information furnished by your company. Enclosed is a copy of the denial letter.
My full name:
My social security number:
My date of birth:
My current address:
My previous address:

Please send the report to the above current address. Thank you.

Your signature

Sample #2: Dispute letter

To: Credit bureau
From: Your name, address, social security number
Date: Today's date
Re: Investigate inaccurate information and remove outdated information

I am disputing the accuracy of the following information on my credit report:
Account name and number—reason
(Example: ABC Store # 23432—I have never had an account with this store please delete from my report. Or, this account was paid and closed a year ago; please update this account.)

Account name and number—reason
I have enclosed copies of paid receipts and letters. The following information is more than seven years old; please remove from my credit report. (Include the account name and number and the last date of activity.)
Please notify me within thirty days when the accounts have been corrected and/or deleted. You may send an updated copy of my credit report to the above address. Also, will you please send me names and addresses of companies you contacted so I may follow up? Your immediate attention will be appreciated. Thank you.

Your signature

Sample #3: Follow-up letter to credit bureau

To: Credit bureau
From: Your name, address, social security number
Date: Today's date
Re: Reminder

Thirty days ago you received my letter disputing the accuracy of several items on my credit report. As of today I have not received a response from you. Attached is a copy of the original letter.

Legally, you are required to respond to my request in thirty days. I assume you were unable to verify the items to be true and accurate; therefore, they must be deleted immediately.

Please send me notification that the items have been deleted and also send an updated copy of my credit report to the above address. Thank you for your immediate attention.

Your signature

Sample #4: Dispute letter to creditor

To: Name of person you spoke to
From: Your name
Date: Today's date
Re: Account number

I am writing this letter to request a change with the credit rating on the above account.

As you know I've had this account for X years and paid the account as agreed until my (divorce, unemployment, illness). I was unable to make timely payments on the account because of the financial crisis I was experiencing. As soon as I was able, I made arrangements and paid the account in full.

My credit rating is important to me for employment and other reasons. It's also important that my credit report reflect my sincere effort to remain a good and loyal customer in spite of an unexpected crisis.

I am requesting that you notify the credit bureaus you report to that my account with you is no longer verifiable. If this is not possible, will you please remove or upgrade the negative rating on this account. I sincerely thank you for your cooperation.

Your signature

Sample #5: Letter to collection agency or creditor to verify agreement

Date
Name and title of person you spoke to
Company name
Address
Re: repayment agreement for account number

Dear (name):

This letter is to confirm our agreement to settle the above account, entered in on (date). The terms we agreed upon were as follows:
- I agree to pay (company) $X per month for X months, due on the X of every month until the account is paid in full.
- The first payment is due (date) and all payments will be mailed to your office located at:

Continue to list the specific terms of agreement you negotiated. Here are some examples:
- If I have a problem making a payment on time and cannot become current within sixty days, I will be in default and the entire balance can be due and payable.
- After six months of on-time payments my account rating will be upgraded.
- Upon final payment of the debt, (company name) will notify credit bureau that this account is no longer verifiable and should be deleted from my credit file.

Will you please confirm the terms of our agreement and sign below? Please call me if there are changes that need to be made. You can mail or fax back to me at the numbers below.
Thank you and I look forward to working with you.

Confirmation of agreement
Signature: _____
Print name: _____
Title: _____

Your name
Address
Telephone number
Fax number

Chapter 13

Protecting Your Credit

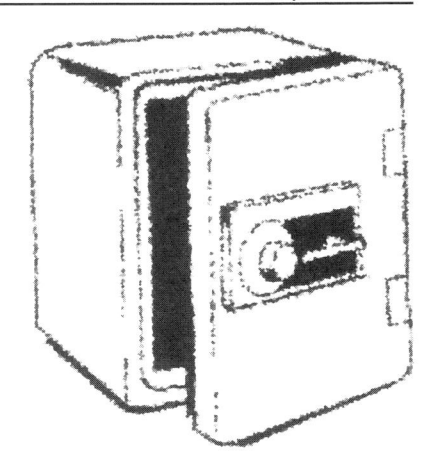

As you can see, your credit rating is a valuable asset for you. You must maintain it and protect it. Do not allow your good credit rating to be borrowed by family or friends like a pair of shoes.

There are two scenarios I have seen destroy credit ratings:

1. A friend or family member asks you to make a major purchase or take out credit in your name and they will make the payments.
2. You are asked to cosign for a friend or family member for a major purchase, usually a car or house.

These requests are made of you for two reasons: the family member or friend does not have an established credit rating or has a bad credit rating.

When you make a purchase or take credit out with the intention that someone else will make the payments, this is your

debt. You can collect the monthly payment from your family member or friend but you must make the payments on time every month. You can't afford to leave the responsibility of maintaining your credit rating to someone else, especially if he or she has not maintained a good credit rating. If you can't afford to make this payment whether or not you receive the payment from the family member or friend, don't do it.

When you cosign for someone you are saying to the lender you will make the payments on this loan if they don't make the payment. The payment history on the account—good or bad—will be reported on both of your credit reports. I have seen cosigned loans ruin so many credit ratings without the knowledge of the cosigner. With cosigned loans, be sure the payments are made on time.

Identity theft is a crime that is on the rise. Identity theft occurs when your name, social security number, and credit card numbers are used without your knowledge to obtain credit in your name. Some ways to protect your credit rating are:

- Be very careful when you give out your social security number. You may request an alternate number be used as an ID in place of your social security number.
- Check your credit card statements for unauthorized purchases.
- Don't give your credit card number to telemarketing companies.
- Use check cards (debit cards) rather than checks, to avoid having your social security number and credit card numbers written on the check.
- Shred or tear up all junk mail, especially pre-approved credit card applications.
- If you have a free-standing mailbox and your mail can be stolen, consider a post office box or a mail slot that deposits your mail directly into your house.

Points to Remember
- A good credit rating is valuable.
- If you use your credit to make a purchase for someone else, be sure you can make the payments.
- If you cosign on a loan, be sure you collect the money and send the payment in on time.
- Check with the lender periodically and see when your name can be removed as a cosigner.
- Protect your social security number.

Part III

Getting Out of Debt

"Debt feels like the heaviest burden of life. It weighs down your spirits, keeps your mind occupied with your burden, and makes you feel bound—because you are bound."

—Suze Orman
The 9 Steps to Financial Freedom

Chapter 14

Strategies to Reduce Debt

Let's skip the discussion of the psychology of debt. To be burdened with a lot of nonessential debt is not good for your physical and mental well being. We are also going to skip the activity of examining every penny you spend on lunch or on a cup of coffee. If you work every day, you should be able to buy lunch or a cup of coffee. After reading this book, you will know when to cut back your spending.

One thing you should know is that reducing your debt is a major step toward financial freedom. In order to reduce your debt, you must manage your money. To manage your money, you need to know three things:

1. How much money do I earn every month?
2. What is the exact amount of my paychecks?
3. How do I spend this money every month?

Write this information down.

I constantly hear people say, "I don't make enough money to manage." I tell them it's not about *how much* you earn, it's what you *do* with how much you earn. I have had the opportunity to review the household economies of hundreds of single individuals and families. I have seen families who earned $35,000 annually accomplish more financially than an individual who earned $60,000 annually. The family kept their debt at a low level and saved as much money as possible. The single individual had a lot of debt and saved very little money.

Let's review the household economy of two single individuals who earn the same amount of money:

Daniel earns $25,000 a year and after taxes brings home approximately $1,500 per month. This is how Daniel's $1,500 is spent every month:

Rent: $400
Utilities: $150
Car insurance: $100
Groceries: $200
Personal expenses (gas, cleaning, entertainment, and so forth):$300
Charitable giving: $100
Credit card: $50
Saving/investing: $200

Daniel is twenty-seven years old and has been on his job for three years. He manages to save an average of $200 per month, sometimes more or less depending on his personal expenses. His car is paid for but he is planning to buy another car within the next year after his annual salary increase. He has been using his savings to pay for car repairs and currently has approximately $5,000 in his money market account. He has one credit card that he uses primarily for emergencies and for small charges he can pay off monthly.

John also earns $25,000 a year and after taxes brings home $1,500 per month. This is how John spends his money every month:

Rent: $400
Utilities: $150
Car insurance: $100
Groceries: $200
Personal expenses (gas, cleaning, entertainment, and so forth): $300
Credit cards: $225
Loans: $125

John is thirty years old and has been on his job for five years. He has a very different lifestyle from Daniel's. He uses his credit for entertainment and clothes. His car is paid for and he also wants a new car. He is up to the credit limit on his credit cards. He has no savings. Two years ago he acquired a consolidation loan for $5,000 to pay off his Visa and MasterCard debt. He owed $2,500 on each card. Consolidating these credit cards into one payment seemed like a good idea because he was paying $100 per month on each card and the loan payment was only $125 per month. Two years later he has a loan payment and the same credit card debt because he did not close the accounts and started to use the cards again. He eventually exhausted his credit limits. He can only make the minimum monthly payments. He is having a difficult time maintaining a good payment history. Without access to his credit lines and no cash reserves, he is headed for disaster.

These are two simple profiles of how two individuals with the same income manage their money. Daniel spends $50 per month on nonessential debt, has cash reserves, available credit, and the ability to handle a financial emergency. John spends $350 per month on nonessential debt and has no cash reserves or available credit. John is in trouble if faced with a financial emergency.

First steps to take to eliminate debt

First you must know exactly whom you owe and how much you owe. Make a list of all your bills with the essential bills on one side and nonessential bills on the other side (see Figure 1 and Sample #6 on page 82). Essential bills are mortgage or rent,

utilities, insurance, child support, student loans, and so forth. These are the ongoing bills you will more than likely continue to pay on a regular basis.
Nonessential bills are the multiple Visa and MasterCard, department store charge cards, gas cards, and so forth.

Looking at the nonessential debt list, separate the installment debt from revolving debt. An installment debt has fixed monthly payments for a specific period of time (such as a car loan). Credit cards, charge cards, line of credit, overdraft protection, and so forth should be listed under revolving debt. List the monthly payments and balances owed on each account. Also, write the last payment date on installment debt.

Figure 1. Nonessential debt

Revolving			Installment			
Visa	50	2,500	Car	350	10,000	8/2002
Visa	75	3,000	Loan	160	1,920	10/2001
MasterCard	125	4,200	Total	$510		
J.C. Penney	100	1,000				
Dillard's	75	800				
Lord & Taylor	130	1,000				
Total	$555					

The total payment on revolving debt is $555 per month, to continue indefinitely. The installment debt is $510 to be reduced to $350 by October of 2001 and paid off completely by August of 2002. There is an end to the installment debt. The focus should be on reducing the revolving debt since there is no end in sight to paying these bills off without a plan.

The goal is to reduce the $555 per month as much and as quickly as possible. You need only one bank card—MasterCard or Visa—with available credit for emergencies, necessities, and convenience. These cards are accepted everywhere and you can get cash advances when you have an emergency and need another source of funds. There is no need for department store charge cards or gas cards as most of these retailers accept MasterCard or Visa. It's much easier to manage your spending with one card. One card with an adequate credit limit can satisfy all your credit needs. To have credit available to you when you need it offers some financial freedom, freedom from worry, and freedom to save and invest your money. To have savings and available credit offers security.

Strategies for reducing and eliminating debt
Do it yourself

This strategy is recommended for individuals who have good credit but too much of it and want to get out of debt. The first challenge is to *stop using the credit cards!* Where do you start? Which bill do you pay off first? Applying the process of systematic reduction and eventual elimination of nonessential debt to Figure 1 will demonstrate how *you* can systemically reduce and ultimately eliminate your debt.

Most money management books encourage you to start with the credit card that charges the highest interest rate. I have a different approach. Because it is imperative for you to see results quickly during this process, I suggest you start with the credit card that has the highest minimum monthly payment with the lowest balance. The goal is to create the largest monthly reduction of debt with the least amount of money.

Start making the minimum monthly payments on all your credit cards. Make all extra payments to the credit card you have selected to pay off first. For example, stop paying $50 extra per month on three different cards and start paying $150 extra on the card you have elected to pay off first. This will accelerate the elimination of the debt.

If necessary, look for sources of extra money such as overtime, part-time work, or your tax refund. It is important that you get the first bill paid off as soon as possible. This is going to allow you to reach your goal of eliminating nonessential debt as quickly as possible.

Let's look at Figure 1 to see how to systematically reduce and eliminate debt. Lord & Taylor would be the first credit card to pay off. Why? The two highest minimum monthly payments are MasterCard at $125 and Lord & Taylor at $130. To eliminate the MasterCard monthly debt it will take $4,200. It will take only $1,000 to pay off the Lord & Taylor account. Making the minimum payment of $130 plus any extra payment can have this bill paid off in six months or less. You have now created $130 per month to apply to eliminating the next bill. By doing this you get the greatest monthly reduction for the least amount of money in the shortest period of time.

Now take the $130 and apply it to the J.C. Penney account. Why? We can free up another $100 per month by only paying off $1,000. By making payments of $100 plus $130 on this account, you will eliminate this bill in approximately five months. In less than a year you have reduced monthly revolving debt by $230 per month. The next bill to eliminate is Dillard's. By this time the balance will be lower and a $305 ($75 plus $100 plus $130) monthly payment should pay this debt off in three months. Now you have reduced your monthly revolving debt payments by $305.

Next will be the Visa card with the $2,500 balance. Your monthly payment of $355 ($50 plus $75 plus $100 plus $130) will eliminate this bill in six months or less. Next will be the other Visa card with a $3,000 balance. Your monthly payments of $430 ($75 plus $50 plus $75 plus $100 plus $130) will eliminate this bill in approximately six months. The final bill to pay off is the MasterCard account with approximately a $4,000 balance. You can now pay $555 ($125 plus $75 plus $50 plus $75 plus $100 plus $130) per month on this card and have it paid off in approximately seven months.

In a relatively short time—thirty-three months—you have systematically eliminated approximately $12,000 in revolving debt while you were continuing to pay the installment debt, which was paid off within the same time period. Now you have no nonessential debt. You have met your goal of continuing to reduce your debt, thereby eliminating it as quickly as possible. You will want to keep one of your bank credit cards—preferably the one with the lowest rate. Now you have the financial freedom to save and invest to meet your financial goals.

This strategy requires discipline and some patience. If you think this a good strategy, but you don't think you have the discipline or patience and you don't mind turning your money over to someone else to manage, perhaps you should consider the next strategy.

Consumer credit counseling services

These are also referred to as debt-management services. The most popular is the nonprofit agency, Consumer Credit Counseling. If you are behind on your bills and have gotten in over your head, this is a good option. These services can sometimes negotiate a reduced payoff of current balances, reduce interest, and lower finance charges. After meeting with a counselor and making out a plan, you are responsible for making the monthly payments to the credit counseling service. Be sure you make these payments on time and watch your statements every month. Make sure your payments are being made according to the agreement with the creditors. Check for late payments. Consumer Credit Counseling and other debt management services' objective is to pay off the creditor according to the terms negotiated.

This service is similar to the do-it-yourself strategy. For example, if you are paying $400 a month to pay on five credit cards and one card is paid off, now you are paying $400 a month to pay off four credit cards, then three, and so on. These services usually cover unsecured debt such as credit cards rather than installment debt such as cars and homes. If you decide to use a debt-management service, make sure you are dealing with a reputable company and compare the service charges and fees. These services will get your bills paid but you may not end up with a good credit history. Their goal is to get you out of debt, not necessarily to repair your credit rating.

Debt consolidation

Through debt consolidation, you borrow enough money to pay off all your bills and make one loan payment, reducing your monthly payment in the process. If you own your home or other real estate, a second mortgage, also called a home equity loan or line of credit, is available to you.

There are several ways to proceed. The most advisable is a home equity line of credit offered by banks to customers with good credit. These loans usually have no closing cost and have an interest rate around the prime lending rate. You can also access additional money when you need it without making a new loan. Here you obtain a second mortgage and leave the first mortgage intact.

Sub-prime lenders will suggest the single-payment scenario, consolidating all your debt into one payment: mortgage, repairs, credit cards, and even some cash for you. Sounds really good, doesn't it? These loans are usually advertised to people with credit problems. Be very careful because the interest rate, fees, and terms can be so outrageous you could lose your home. This solution consolidates the first mortgage with your other debts. So, you could conceivably start with a first mortgage of $50,000, for example, and end up with a first mortgage of $100,000.

If you don't own a home, there are credit unions that offer up to $7,500 loans with no collateral, only your signature and meeting the other qualifications are required. This is usually an installment loan requiring a good credit history. I don't recommend finance companies to consolidate debt because the interest rate and finance charges are too high. Be sure the amount you can get will be enough to pay off all your bills, or it may not be worth it. For example, you can get a signature loan for $3,000, but to consolidate all your bills you need $6,000. Ask yourself, am I reducing my total monthly payments as much as I can and as quickly as possible?

Personal bankruptcy

When you find yourself threatened with a foreclosure, wage garnishment, calls from bill collectors, loss of employment, or serious illness, or if you are in so much debt that you see no way of ever being able to repay your debt—when you have exhausted all your options, this is the remedy of last resort. The decision to file bankruptcy is a legal procedure with long-term effects on your financial independence and should not be taken lightly.

There are two types of personal bankruptcies: Chapter 13 and Chapter 7.

Caution: If you are filing bankruptcy to discharge delinquent child support, student loans, or delinquent taxes, you may not be able to discharge these debts by filing a Chapter 7. Be sure to consult an attorney because Chapter 13 might be the only option.

Chapter 13 is also known as the wage earner's plan. Some attorneys market Chapter 13 as a debt-consolidation plan. I know of people who have filed Chapter 13 and didn't know they had filed bankruptcy. Chapter 13 allows you to keep your assets and pay back your creditors in three to five years, usually through payroll deductions.

Chapter 7 is also known as a straight bankruptcy. It requires liquidation of all assets that are not exempt in your state. Each state has bankruptcy laws that exempt or protect certain assets from bankruptcy, such as work-related tools, household furnishings, and some equity in property. There are federal- and state-exempt bankruptcy laws. Some states will allow you to choose and others will not. After your assets are liquidated and the creditors are paid with the proceeds, the bankruptcy is discharged. This discharges your debts and generally the creditors can no longer try to collect any unpaid obligation from you.

After bankruptcy, be sure to get a copy of your credit report and follow the steps for repairing and reestablishing your credit rating.

Don't file for bankruptcy and change your mind. Because it is a legal procedure, it will still show up in public records that you filed even if you didn't go through with it.

Points to Remember
- What you do with what you earn is just as important as how much you earn.
- There is essential debt and nonessential debt.
- It's important to write down your bills and list them in the appropriate category.
- The goal is to reduce the nonessential debt as quickly as possible.
- To accomplish this goal you can utilize one of these strategies: (1) do it yourself, (2) consumer credit counseling, (3) debt consolidation, or (4) legal bankruptcy.

Sample #6:

Essential debt	**Non-essential debt**

Part IV

Credit and Purchasing a Home

" . . . keep moving in the direction of your dreams"

—*Thoreau*

Chapter 15

A Stress-Free Loan Process

The American dream has turned into a nightmare. Record numbers of foreclosures and loss of value have made many Americans question the value of homeownership. However, with interest rates being the lowest in history, sale prices more affordable, and rental rates rising, for many it costs less to own than to rent. Millions of dollars continue to change hands every day for financing the purchase of homes. For those who are taking the plunge into homeownership, financing the American dream can be a joyous, stressful, frustrating, or disappointing experience. Getting approved for a home loan is much more difficult today. Your credit score is one major factor.

Lenders must determine what level of risk your credit history represents before a decision can be made. Lenders look very favorably on applicants who are paying their debts as agreed now and in the past. Applicants who have had difficulties will require more attention to determine the reason for the poor credit history. If there are valid extenuating circumstances (loss of income, illness, divorce, death, and so forth), the applicant can still receive favorable consideration.

If you have not established a credit history, you will need to do so. Some alternative sources of credit are rent, telephone, gas, electric, cable television, and insurance payments. If you can provide documentation to show a good payment history to at least three or four of these accounts for one year, you will be given favorable consideration. If you can't establish an alternative credit history, consideration becomes less favorable.

However, the fact still remains that a good credit history entitles you to the best interest rates, low documentation, a variety of loan products, faster decisions, lower cost, and the best customer service. A poor credit history and sometimes no credit history will get you denied or subject you to higher interest rates, undesirable loan terms, higher cost, extra documentation, a large cash investment, and a much slower decision process.

Let's examine the areas reviewed by lenders.

Qualification

What is the source of your income? Is it likely to continue? Does your current income support the proposed mortgage payment and your current monthly obligations? As a general rule of thumb, the proposed house payment (principal and interest on the loan, real estate taxes, homeowner's insurance, and mortgage insurance) should not exceed 29 percent of your gross monthly income (income before taxes). Your total debt, including the proposed house payment, should not exceed 36 to 38 percent of your gross monthly income. Some loan products, such as FHA and VA loans, have a total debt ratio of 41 percent of your gross monthly income.

For instance, if you have a gross monthly income of $3,000 and monthly debt of $400, your maximum allowable house payment is $680, using a total debt ratio of 36 percent. If your debt were $200 per month, your allowable housing payment would increase to $870. The math process would be $3,000 x 29% = $870; $870 + $400 = $1,270, or 42% total debt. This house payment would be lowered to $680 to qualify at both 29% and 36%. If your debt were $200 per month, then $3,000 x 29% = $870; $870 + $200 = $1,070, or 36% total debt. If you use the total debt ratio of 41 percent with $400 of monthly debt, your maximum allowable house payment would be $830. If your debt were $200 per month, your maximum housing expense would increase to only $870.00 because with a 41 percent total debt ratio you are allowed to carry more debt without affecting your house payment ratio of 29 percent.

Note: With a good credit score and more than a minimum down payment, some lenders will waive the debt-to-income ratio requirement.

Documentation required. You'll need the last two years' W-2 forms, most recent thirty-day paycheck stubs, and two years' residential history (landlord name, address, and telephone number). Self-employed applicants need the last two years' tax returns (your net income, not your gross income, is used for qualifying purposes).

Closing funds

Do you have the money for down payment and closing costs? Can the money be verified in a bank account or investment account? Minimum down payments can range from 3 to 5 percent of the purchase price. Closing costs, depending on where in the country you live, can equal or exceed the minimum down payment amount.

Note: There are specific requirements for funds to close. Check with your lender on the following: (1) seasoning requirements for funds used for closing (the length of time the money has been in the bank), (2) gifts from family members, and (3) down payment assistance programs.

Documentation required. You'll need the most recent two months' bank statements or most recent investment statements.

The credit report

To obtain a mortgage, you'll need a report that has the credit history from the three credit-reporting agencies, called a three-merge credit report. This is to ensure the lender is getting all your credit information. The credit report must be up-to-date with current terms, balances, and ratings for accounts listed on the loan application. Your application and the credit report should match.

A public record search for each city the borrower has lived in for the last two to seven years to disclose any judgments, foreclosures, garnishments, bankruptcies, or divorce actions is also required.

Joint credit reports are obtained for married couples. Individual reports are obtained for unmarried applicants and newly married couples. When reviewing the credit report, the lender pays close attention to the following specific areas:

- ***Slow payments.*** When did the slow payments occur, in the past or recently? How many accounts? Were these isolated incidents or is this a pattern? Are there collection accounts, judgments, or charge-offs? Are they paid? How long ago where they paid? A decision should not be rendered without giving you the opportunity to provide a written explanation.

- ***Undisclosed debt.*** Does the credit report reveal significant debt that the borrower did not disclose on the loan application? This is viewed as an indication that the borrower is trying to conceal his or her true financial picture. Sometimes there are good reasons for this occurring. For instance, if there was a divorce and the ex-spouse is responsible for the payment, it was not listed (You must have documentation to support this.); or there was a bankruptcy and the credit report was never cleaned up to show what debts were included; or it could simply be an error. That is why you should get a copy of your credit report before applying for a mortgage. You want to avoid unpleasant surprises.

- ***Revolving accounts.*** All revolving accounts must show minimum payments; if they don't, the lender will count 5 percent of the unpaid balance as a payment. If you have a credit card with a $4,000 balance, without a minimum payment on your credit report the payment counted against you will be $200, even though your actual payment is $120. This could affect your qualifying for the loan. Provide copies of your statements showing the minimum monthly payment.

Credit score

Mortgage lenders are relying on credit scores more and more to eliminate bias. According to some lenders, this is the most expedient and objective way to determine credit risk. Generally, the level of risk falls into the following categories:

- A score of 700 and above represents a low risk of default. These applicants have an acceptable credit history.
- A score of 640 through 660 begins to represent a higher degree of default risk. A decision will not be made on credit score alone. The lender will look to other areas of the loan application to strengthen the file, such as assets and debt-to-income ratios.
- A score below 620 represents a statistically high risk of default. This applicant's application will be looked at very carefully before a decision can be made. Credit history will be carefully scrutinized. Other areas of the file, such as assets, debt-to-income ratio, and extenuating circumstances will be examined. The applicant may be referred to a subprime lender.

As you can see, a credit score of less than 620 can make obtaining the best financing for a home difficult. However, there are alternatives:

- If the low credit score is due to lack of credit usage, provide alternative credit sources.
- If the low credit score is due to extenuating circumstances, write a letter and provide all the documentation you can to support your reasons.
- Try an FHA loan or Freddie Mac and Fannie Mae affordable loan products. More of these loans are made with lower credit scores.
- Make a larger down payment.

If all else fails, it's best to wait, clean up your credit, and try again later.

Mortgage/rental history

This is very important to your loan application. If you have recent late payments without a good reason, this can cause an automatic decline.

Judgments, collections, or liens

These should be paid in full prior to making loan application with satisfactory letter of explanation and good reestablished credit. If for some reason you apply and discover you have unpaid judgments or collections, some lenders will allow you to pay them prior to closing as long as your current credit is good. You must have a letter of explanation, documentation, and verifiable funds to pay them.

Delinquent child support

If child support shows on your credit report as a judgment or collection, it generally must be paid in order to get a clear title to the property.

Garnishments

Most lenders will allow for child support payments coming directly from paychecks. All other creditor garnishments must be paid.

Foreclosure/repossession

Generally lenders will not approve a loan if the applicant has had a mortgage foreclosure in the last three years of his or her credit history. If it has been three or more years and there were extraordinary circumstances beyond the control of the applicant, and the applicant's current employment and credit situation are such that the events that caused the foreclosure are not likely to recur, the applicant can be given favorable consideration. The same applies for repossessions.

Tax liens

These must be paid. Some lenders will allow you to show proof of a payment plan and count the payment as a monthly obligation.

Consumer credit counseling service (CCC)

If you are currently enrolled in such a service, a twelve-month payment history showing no late payments is required. If you have completed the program within the last twelve months, evidence of a satisfactory payment history is still required. One area to watch for with debt-management services is you may have made your payments to them as agreed but the creditors continue to report late payments. Therefore, your credit report shows late payments. Be prepared to show evidence that you always paid the counseling service on time. You may have a problem with this if you have bills you are paying that were not included in CCC and they also show late payments. If you are paying your bills late you can't blame late payments on Consumer Credit Counseling services.

Bankruptcy

The bankruptcy should be fully discharged two to four years from the mortgage application date. Applicant should have re-established good credit and demonstrated an ability to manage their financial affairs. Be prepared to provide a written explanation for filing bankruptcy and a copy of the full bankruptcy papers showing the schedule of debts. Chapter 13 bankruptcy has the same requirements; however you may be able to apply for a mortgage one year after the discharge date with some loan products.

Credit explanation letters

When applying for a mortgage and you have had credit problems, most lenders require letters of explanations concerning your credit issues. When writing these letters, be truthful, precise; provide documented proof to support your explanation;

state why the credit problems occurred and what you have done to prevent them from recurring. Good letters of explanation can make the difference between a loan approval and denial.

Points to Remember
- To obtain an approval for a mortgage loan you must qualify for the amount of money you want to borrow, have money saved or approved sources for the down payment and closing costs, and show a good credit rating for the last twelve to twenty-four months.
- Credit scores pay a major role in mortgage lending.
- Review your credit report prior to applying for a mortgage.
- Clear up any potential problems.
- Provide documentation for any past credit problems.
- Be prepared to write letters of explanation of any credit problems.
- Be prepared with most recent W-2 forms, paycheck stubs, bank statements, and tax returns (if applicable).
- If you have no credit history, get credit letters showing a good payment history from your landlord, telephone, gas, electric, cable, or insurance company.

Conclusion

Congratulations! You have completed the journey and obtained a broad, basic knowledge of credit and debt. I hope I've been able to shed some light on an important area of your life that can easily be neglected. I have tried to provide information you can use to reduce your debt and improve your credit rating and standard of living.

It is ironic that while I was writing this conclusion, I observed a segment of the evening news that addressed the issue of college students who had bad credit and lots of debt before finishing college. One student was forced to drop out of school and start working full-time to pay her debts. Eleven years later, she had not gone back to school. Another student had decided not to go to graduate school; instead he was going to get a job to pay off his debt. Young people in their twenties are filing for bankruptcy. Many of us are working jobs we do not like because we have bills to pay. We are making bad choices because we are in desperate situations and feel we have no other choice. These are life-hanging decisions based on credit and debt.

You can see just how important credit is to your life and how necessary it is for you to have good credit and very little debt. We are quickly approaching a cashless society and credit is so powerful. If you don't have access to credit, you will be living on the fringes of society. Have you ever tried to book a flight, rent a car, or reserve a hotel room without a credit card? Good credit and low debt allow you the freedom to live the life you want to live.

I recommend you do two things: First, position yourself in this economy with good credit, so you have access to credit whenever there is a need. Whether it is investing for your retirement, starting a business, obtaining employment, purchasing a home, or obtaining a credit card, good credit is essential.

Second, lower your debt (and start saving that money) and keep it low enough to manage if you lost your job or took a pay cut (either forced or voluntary).

I hope the information is this book has empowered you to act and make some of your dreams come true. Do it for yourself. Do it for your children.

Resources

Web sites

www.myfico.com
www.creditboards.com
www.creditinsider.com
www.bankrate.com
www.mint.com
www.makinghomeaffordable.com
www.annualcreditreport.com
www.ftc.gov
www.hud.gov

Publications

Amos, Orley, M. Jr., *Economic Literacy*, Hawthorne, New Jersey, Career Press, 1994.
Burkett, Larry, *Victory Over Debt*, Chicago, Illinois, Northfield Publishing, 1992.
Chatzky, Jean, *You Don't Have to Be Rich*, New York, New York, Portfolio, 2003.
Weston, Liz Pulliam, *Your Credit Score*, New Jersey, FT Press, 2007.

Government agencies

Federal Trade Commission
Consumer Response Center-FCRA
Washington, DC 20580
Questions and concerns: Credit-reporting agencies and creditors

Federal Reserve Board
Division of Consumer and Community Affairs
Washington, DC 20551
Questions and concerns: Federal Reserve System member banks except national banks and federal branch agencies of foreign banks

Federal Deposit Insurance Corporation
Division of Compliance and Consumer Affairs
Washington, DC 20429
Questions and concerns: State-chartered banks that are not members of the Federal Reserve System

Office of the Comptroller of the Currency
Compliance Management, Mail Stop 6-6; Washington, DC 20219
Questions and concerns: National banks, federal branch agencies of foreign banks—the word "National" or initials "N.A." appear in or after bank's name

Office of Thrift Supervision
Consumer Programs
Washington, DC 20552
Questions and concerns: Savings associations and federally chartered savings bank—the word "federal" or initials "F.S.B." appear in the institution's name

National Credit Union Administration
1775 Duke Street; Alexandria, VA 22314
Questions and concerns: Federal credit unions—the words "federal credit union" appear in the institution's name

Terms You Need to Know

Annual percentage rate (APR)—the percentage cost of credit on a yearly basis.

Assets—something of value that you own. For an individual or family, assets can be financial, such as money, stocks, bonds, bank accounts or it can be physical, such as houses, cars, boats, land, jewelry, and so forth.

Bankruptcy—to legally declare that you are unable to pay the bills you are liable for. Bankruptcy is governed by federal laws. The options for personal bankruptcy are Chapter 7, which allows individuals or businesses to liquidate or sell assets and distribute to creditors, and Chapter 13, which allows a payment plan for an individual's debt.

Capital—money (savings account, stocks, bonds, and so forth) and property (houses, land, and so forth) that one owns.

Capitalism—an economic system characterized by private or corporate ownership of capital goods; by investments that are determined by private decision rather than by state control; and by prices, production, and the distribution of goods that are determined mainly by competition in a free market.

Cash advance—use your credit card at a bank or ATM to get a cash loan. The interest rate is higher than purchases, and there are additional fees and usually no grace period.

Charge card—requires you pay your bill in full every month, but charges no interest. Examples: American Express or Diners Club.

Close—term used in mortgage financing meaning to finalize the purchase by signing all legal documents for transferring of ownership of real estate.

Collateral—property used to support a loan and subject to seizure if you default on the loan. Also called security.

Consumer—you.

Consumer Credit Protection Act—federal regulations of credit activities, such as FCRA and FDCPA.

Consumer statement—an up to one-hundred word statement you can add to your credit report explaining your side of a disputed credit report entry.

Cosigner—another person who signs on your loan and assumes equal responsibility for it.

Credit—the promise to pay in the future in exchange for money, goods, or services you receive in the present. Credit cards, mortgages, and car loans are all forms of credit.

Credit bureaus—also called consumer reporting agencies; these are not government agencies. They must comply with federal authorities and laws that oversee their operations. Credit bureaus are just like any other business. They buy and sell information and services for a profit.

Credit card—allows you to make partial payments for purchases but charges interest on the amount owed. Balances can be paid in full to avoid interest payments. Visa, MasterCard and retail store cards are credit cards.

Credit file—all the information the credit bureaus have on you to create a credit report.

Credit history—a record of what you have borrowed and how you have paid.

Credit report—also known as consumer reports and credit checks. A written summary of your credit history.

Credit score—a statistical system used to determine if a person is creditworthy.

Creditor—an individual or business from whom you borrow or to whom you owe money.

Creditworthy—a creditor's determination of an individual's ability and willingness to repay debts.

Debt—an amount owed, an obligation.

Debt to income ratio—percentage of income that is owed, excluding some essential obligations such as utilities and insurance.

Debtor—one who owes the debt.

Default—failure to repay a debt or meet the terms of the agreement.

Discharged—the elimination of debt through bankruptcy.

Electronic Fund Transfer Act (EFTA)—establishes procedures for electronic fund transfer account statement. This act applies to electronic fund transfer, such as automatic teller machines, point-of-sale debit transactions (debit cards), and other electronic banking transactions.

Equal Credit Opportunity Act (ECOA)—prohibits credit discrimination on the basis of sex, race, marital status, religion, national origin, age, or receipt of public assistance.

Essential debt—a monthly obligation that is likely to continue such as rent/mortgage, utilities, child support, and so forth. Liabilities that produce income such as investments can also be an essential debt.

Fair Credit Billing Act (FCBA)—establishes procedures for resolving mistakes on credit billing. This act generally applies only to "open-end" credit accounts—credit cards, revolving charge accounts such as department store accounts and overdraft checking accounts. Does not apply to loans or other installment debts.

Fair Credit Reporting Act (FCRA)—a public law designed to help ensure that credit-reporting agencies furnish correct and complete information to businesses to use when evaluating your application.

Fair Debt Collection Practices Act (FDCPA)—prohibits debt collectors from engaging in unfair, deceptive, or abusive practices while collecting these debts. The act applies to personal, family, and household debts. It includes money owed for the purchase of a car, medical care, or deceptive or abusive practices while collecting these debts.

Fannie Mae—a private shareholder-owned company that works to make sure mortgage money is available for people in communities all across America. Fannie Mae does not lend money directly to home buyers but works with lenders to make sure mortgage funds are available.

Federal Housing Administration (FHA)—a Housing and Urban Development operation that insures private lenders against losses on mortgage financing and multifamily housing.

Federal Trade Commission (FTC)—enforces credit laws that protect your right to obtain, use, and maintain credit. These laws do not guarantee that everyone will receive credit. The credit laws protect your rights by requiring businesses to give all consumers a fair and equal opportunity to receive credit and to resolve disputes over credit errors.

FICO (Fair, Isaac and Co.)—the company that created the generic credit score. Examples of FICO scores are the Beacon score, the Empirica score, and FICO.

Finance charge—the total dollar amount that credit costs. Includes interest cost, service charges, and optional credit-related insurance premiums. For example, if you borrow $100 for a year at $10 interest and service chare of $3, the finance charge would be $13.

Freddie Mac—a stockholder-owned corporation chartered by Congress in 1970 to create a continuous flow of funds to mortgage lenders in support of homeownership and rental housing. Freddie Mac purchases mortgages from lenders and packages them into securities that are sold to investors.

Garnishment—the attachment of wages to satisfy a debt.

Grace period—with installment debt, period of time beyond the due date that a late payment will not be charged. For example, a mortgage payment due on the 1st of the month that doesn't charge a late payment until after the 16th of the month. With credit cards, it is the number of days you have before a credit card company begins to charge you interest on your new purchases.

Housing and Urban Development (HUD)—executive branch of government that oversees home mortgage lending, creates affordable rental housing, stimulates community and economic development, and enforces fair housing laws.

Inquiries—name of creditors who have checked into your credit.

Installment debt—accounts with a fixed monthly payment for a specific period of time until the account is paid. For example, a car loan with a monthly payment of $330 for forty-eight months is an installment loan.

Investigative consumer reports—detailed reports that involve interviews with your neighbors or acquaintances about your lifestyle, character, and reputation. This type of report may be used in connection with insurance and employment applications. You'll be notified in writing when a company orders such a report. The notice will explain your rights to request certain information about the report from the company you have made application to. If your application is rejected, you may get additional information from the credit-reporting agency. However, the credit-reporting agency does not have to reveal the sources of the information.

Joint account—a credit account held by two or more people, all can use the account and all assume legal responsibility to repay.

Late payments—payments made after the due date of credit agreement.

Liability—a legal responsibility to repay a debt.

Nonessential debt—unnecessary monthly obligations such as duplicate credit cards.

Obsolete information—negative information on a credit report beyond the legal time limit, usually seven years (ten years for bankruptcy).

Open-end credit—a line of credit that may be used over and over again. This includes credit cards, overdraft protection accounts, and home equity lines of credit.

Predatory lending—abusive lending practices aimed at people with credit problems and limited credit options.

Public record—legal events that are related to your creditworthiness, such as bankruptcy or judgments.

Secured loan—a loan that requires some type of collateral such as savings account, real estate, stocks, certificates of deposits, and so forth.

Three C's—what creditors refer to in determining creditworthiness.
- Capacity. Can you afford the debt you want to take on?
- Character. How is your track record for repaying your debts?
- Collateral. Is the creditor fully protected if you fail to repay?

Unsecured loan—a loan that does not require collateral, only your signature.

Index

A
Abusive loan practices 29-31
Acceptable credit score 22
Accounts 8, 13, 18, 19, 21, 37, 55-60, 64, 75, 78, 86, 88, 89
Advance fee loan 31
Alternative credit 86, 89
Asset 67, 93, 100, 103
Attorney General 11, 50

B
Background information 11, 13, 15, 16, 56
Bankruptcy 7, 12, 13, 18, 23, 26, 27, 41, 56, 88, 91, 93
   Chapter 13 80, 81, 92
   Chapter 7 80, 81
   credit reporting 11, 12, 17, 25
   discharge 80, 81, 91, 92
Business credit 3, 4, 6, 12, 53, 94

C
Capitalism 5, 6
Cash advance 76
Charge cards 76
Check card 68
Checking account 36
Child support 13, 76, 80, 90
Code 15, 17, 18, 19, 40, 56
Collateral 80
Collection agencies 13, 14, 45, 60, 66
Collections 13, 19, 23, 46, 54, 90
Consolidating debt 75, 80
Consumer ads 54
Consumer credit counseling 46, 79, 81, 91
Consumer report. *See* Credit report
Consumer rights 12, 25, 41
Consumer statement 26, 41, 42, 60, 62
Cosign 13, 17, 19, 67-69
Counseling 40, 46, 79, 81, 91
Credit 1, 3-9, 11-19, 21-27, 29-31, 33, 35, 36, 37, 39-43, 45, 46, 47, 48, 49, 51, 53-69, 74-81, 83, 85-95, 105
   divorce 8, 53, 65, 86, 88
   employment 5, 8, 9, 13, 16, 25, 26, 41, 47, 53, 56, 65, 80, 91, 94
   stress 7, 9, 85
Credit bureau 11-15, 19, 22, 25, 26, 27, 37, 41, 42, 54-65
Credit cards 8, 12, 13, 23, 37, 75-80, 86
Credit check. *See* Credit report
Credit explanation 92
Credit file 12, 13, 25, 26, 41, 54, 61, 66
Credit history 9, 12-16, 18, 19, 21, 36, 37, 39, 54, 59, 60, 79, 80, 85, 86, 88, 89, 91, 92
Credit references 37
Credit repair 13, 39-43
   sample letters 63-66
Credit Repair Organization Act 39-43
Credit report 8, 11-15, 17, 18, 19, 22-27, 37, 41, 54-65, 68, 81, 88-92
Credit reporting agency 17
Credit score 21-24, 53, 87, 89, 90, 92

D
Debit cards 68
Debt 4-9, 17-19, 21, 23, 36, 37, 40, 45-51, 53, 60, 66, 68, 71, 73-82, 85-89, 91-94
Debt collector 45, 46, 50, 51

Debt consolidation 79, 81
Debt management service 79
Debt to income ratio 86, 87
Delinquent 54, 90
Delinquent credit 54, 80
Delinquent taxes 80
Discharged 81, 91

E
Employment 5, 8, 9, 12, 13, 16, 25, 26, 41, 47, 53, 56, 65, 80, 91, 94
Equal Credit Opportunity Act 17
Essential debt 73, 75-78, 81, 82

F
Fair Credit Reporting Act 11, 25
Fair Debt Collection Practice Act 45, 48, 50
Fannie Mae 30, 90
Federal Trade Commission 11, 39, 42, 50
FHA 30, 86, 90
FICO 22
Finance charge 3, 29, 79, 80
Foreclosure 13, 18, 30, 61, 80, 88, 91
Freddie Mac 90
Funds 76, 87, 90

G
Garnishment 48, 50, 80, 88, 90
Gas card 76

H
High credit 16
Historical status 13
History 9, 12-16, 18, 19, 21, 36, 37, 39, 40, 54, 58-62, 68, 75, 79, 80, 85-92
Home loan 23
    credit 23-24
Household economy 3, 4, 74

I
Individual account 8, 17, 19
Individual production 5
Inquiries 14, 18, 54
Installment debt 76, 78, 79
Insufficient credit file 54, 61

J
Joint account 8, 17
Judgment 12, 13, 18, 19, 23, 46, 49, 54, 61, 88, 90

L
Liability 8, 17, 49
Line of credit 17, 76, 79
Loan flipping 30, 31

M
Major credit bureau 12, 55
Manner of payment 17
MasterCard 36, 37, 75-78
Money management 77
Mortgage history 90

N
National economy 3
Non-essential debt 82
Notice of Cancellation 42

O
Old information 56

P
Points 4, 6, 8, 9, 14, 19, 21, 22, 24, 27, 30, 31, 37, 43, 51, 56, 60, 62, 69, 81, 92
Predatory lending 29, 30
Prepayment penalty 30
Private ownership 5, 6
Public record 13, 18, 19, 81, 88

Q
Qualifying 53, 87, 89

R
Revolving accounts 89

S
Secured credit card 36, 37
Slow payments 88
Sub-prime loan 30
Symbol 15, 19, 47

T
Tax lien 13, 61, 91

U
Undisclosed debt 88
Unsecured credit 36, 37
Use of credit 4-6, 24

V
Verifiable funds 90
Visa 36, 37, 75, 76, 78, 79, 105

Give the Gift of
The Secrets to Good Credit and Debt Reduction
to Your Friends and Colleagues

CHECK YOUR LEADING BOOKSTORE OR ORDER HERE

❏ **YES**, I want _____ copies of *The Secrets to Good Credit and Debt Reduction* at $12.00 each, plus $4 shipping per book, $.50 for each additional copy (Missouri residents please add $.90 sales tax per book). Canadian orders must be accompanied by a postal money order in U.S. funds. Allow 15 days for delivery.

My check or money order for $_____ is enclosed.

For Office Use: Date_____ Filled_____ Shipped_____

Name _____

Organization _____

Address _____

City/State/Zip _____

Phone_____ E-mail _____

Please make your check payable and return to:
Premier Educational Services, LLC
PO Box 771491
St. Louis, MO 63177

Fax: 314-588-1616 • *Email:* deborah.smartsolutions@gmail.com